EXPLORING THE ANCIENT WORLD

AA

EXPLORING THE ANCIENT WORLD

A GUIDE TO THE MOST OUTSTANDING HISTORICAL WONDERS EVER BUILT

DR PAUL BAHN

AA

© Automobile Association Developments Limited 2008
Relief Map Images supplied by Mountain High Maps®
Copyright© 1993 Digital Wisdom, Inc.

First published 2008

ISBN: 978 0 7495 5864 2
ISBN: Special Sales 978 0 7495 5886 4

Published by AA Publishing, a trading name of Automobile
Association Developments Limited, whose registered office is Fanum
House, Basing View, Basingstoke, Hampshire RG21 4EA. Registered
number 1878835.

A CIP catalogue record for this book is available from the British
Library

Contributing authors: Paul Bahn, Caroline Bird, Peter Bogucki, Phil
Duke, David Gill, Enrique Lopez, Jane McIntosh, Elena Miklashevich,
Gina Muskett, Campbell Price, Margarete Prüch, Anne Solomon
Design and artwork by Andrew Milne Design Ltd
Picture research by Lesley Grayson
Image retouching and repro by Sarah Montgomery
Editorial management by Apostrophe S Ltd
Colour separation by Imaging MM, London
Printed in China by C&C Offset Printing Co., Ltd.
Production by Stephanie Allen

A03643

CONTENTS

INTRODUCTION

Below: Chichén Itzá, Mexico

Archaeological tourism is constantly increasing in popularity, and is an economic factor of considerable importance in many parts of the world, such as Egypt, Peru or Easter Island. Exploring the ancient world is a growth industry, and the primary purpose of this book is simply to present a tiny sample of the enormous variety of sites which can be visited by the archaeological tourist.

Readers will find a mixture of extremely famous, much-visited sites and others that may be totally new to them. This is not merely to show the tourist that there is more to the past than Stonehenge and the Pyramids. It may also help to relieve the pressure on the most popular sites. Just a few decades ago, only the very wealthy could even imagine visiting sites abroad, let alone in the most remote and exotic parts of the world. Yet today it has become commonplace for the man in the street, the student and even the gap-year teenager to travel to other continents, thanks to relatively cheap air travel.

One of the basic dilemmas confronting archaeologists and the custodians of ancient sites is how to balance the public's right to visit our common heritage with the necessity to protect the sites for future generations; for we do not really own these sites, we are merely their caretakers. Our grandchildren and their grandchildren will want to see these same places. Yet many countries, especially but not exclusively in the Third World, are in such desperate need of the income earned by archaeological tourism that they permit numbers of visitors which are hugely excessive and that can often do damage to the fabric of the sites. Places such as Angkor Wat and the Valley of the Kings are constantly awash with crowds, a fact that diminishes their emotional impact and the enjoyment of visiting them. But there are, fortunately, countless ancient sites where one can still be alone, or almost alone, which is a remarkable and often emotional or spiritual experience.

We have tried to provide examples from many different corners of the world, since tourism has become so global in its coverage. However, we reluctantly decided to omit countries such as Iraq, though rich in major archaeological sites, which are unlikely to be accessible to tourism for some time to come.

We have also endeavoured to present sites of many different kinds—temples and tombs, monuments and monasteries, rock art, cities and buffalo jumps. Far from focusing entirely on rulers and huge constructions, the study of the ancient past also investigates the everyday lives of ordinary people, from hunter-gatherers to peasants, from slaves to artisans. Archaeology is an incredibly vast and varied field, encompassing everything from wrecks at the bottom of the sea to frozen children on Andean peaks. Obviously these extremes cannot possibly be visited by the tourist, and nor can sites of difficult physical access, such as most decorated caves.

Nevertheless, that still leaves us with an immense range of accessible sites—and any of the specialists who have contributed to this volume could easily have filled it with examples from their area of expertise:

Below: Getting a good view of the Great Zimbabwe ruins, near the Masvingo, Zimbabwe

Egypt, the Maya, the Classical World, and so forth. Each of them therefore had to make some very difficult choices, to select a varied handful of visitable places of different kinds.

At the time of writing, a Finnish man has just been prosecuted for pulling off part of the ear of a statue on Easter Island, which he presumably wanted as a souvenir, or perhaps to sell on the web. Fortunately the piece he broke off was a modern fragment, which had been attached to the original to complete it, but he did not know that. As astounding as this act of vandalism may seem, it is merely one end of a spectrum of behaviour, some of which may seem comparatively innocuous, for example, removing a potsherd that one might find at one's feet on a site, or a bit of bone or a little stone tool.

But nothing should ever be removed from an archaeological site, and of course one should never drop litter on them either (or indeed anywhere). To use the old cliché, leave only footprints, take away only photos and memories. Moreover, the buying of antiquities is equally taboo. Many sites are surrounded by stalls or hawkers selling replicas and souvenirs of all kinds, a practice that is encouraged since it helps the local economy. But anyone purporting to sell authentic antiquities should be shunned completely, and indeed reported to the authorities—even if the items are actually modern fakes. Nothing is more damaging

Right: An archaeologist gently brushes sand away from a ceramic artefact, Amarna, Egypt

Above: Ahu Tongariki, Easter Island, west of Chile, South America

to the preservation and study of the human past than the plundering of tombs and settlements for art objects or precious metals that can be sold to collectors for inflated prices. The past belongs to everyone, and so the illegal unearthing of an antiquity is a theft from all of us.

The buying of a single illegally obtained object merely serves to feed the monster, the antiquities trade, which has already caused the destruction of countless sites and tombs all over the world. In the process of extracting the 'desirables' from the earth, the robbers obliterate their archaeological context, casting aside the pots or bones or other materials that are of no saleable value. The information lost is vast and irreplaceable.

The future of archaeology—and therefore of archaeological tourism—depends to a very large extent on establishing a fundamental respect for the past. Above all, the education of the young is absolutely crucial, and television programmes as well as specialized books and magazines (such as *DIG* in the USA), aimed at youngsters, are playing a fundamental role in ensuring that future generations will still have archaeological monuments to visit, and that new discoveries will continue to be made. We hope that this book will help to show people that visiting a wide array of archaeological sites is a rich and rewarding experience.

WORLD SITE LOCATOR

SEVEN WONDERS OF THE WORLD

THE IDEA OF SEVEN 'WONDERS' OR 'AMAZING THINGS' WAS FORMULATED IN THE 2ND CENTURY BC. THEY WERE RECORDED BY ANTIPATER OF SIDON (WHO WROTE AN EPIGRAM ON THE DESTRUCTION OF CORINTH BY ROMAN FORCES IN 146BC). THE ORIGINAL RANGE OF SIGHTS WAS CENTRED IN THE EASTERN MEDITERRANEAN AND MESOPOTAMIA.

Below: Aerial view of the pyramid of Menkaure, smallest of the Giza pyramids in Egypt

WONDERS IN EGYPT, BABYLON AND GREECE

The Pyramids on the Giza plateau were the only monument in Egypt. These had become part of the sacred landscape of Ptolemaic Egypt and continue to draw visitors today. Two of the ancient wonders were in Babylon: the city walls and the gardens of the 9th-century BC Semiranis, wife of Shamshi-Adad V of Assyria. There was one 'wonder' in mainland Greece: the colossal gold and ivory chryselephantine statue of Olympian Zeus. This had been made for the earlier temple of Zeus at Olympia by the Athenian sculptor Pheidias probably in the late 430s BC. Remains of his workshop (turned into a later Byzantine church) can still be seen at Olympia; this had the same dimensions and orientation as the cella (or inner room) of the temple where the statue was to be placed. The statue was removed to Byzantium (Istanbul) where it was displayed in the Palace of Lausus. Although lost, it has been suggested that the bearded face of Christ Pantokrator or 'ruler of the world' in the roof of the basilica of Hagia Sophia in Istanbul may have been inspired by the Zeus.

EPHESUS: THE TEMPLE OF ARTEMIS

The Temple of Artemis at the Greek city of Ephesus in western Turkey can be traced back to the archaic period (6th century BC). Indeed there is a historical tradition that the famously rich King Kroisos dedicated columns in the sanctuary. The structure was huge with a length of some 115m (377ft), and a width of over 55m (180ft). It was surrounded by multiple rows of columns, perhaps giving the architectural impression of walking through a forest before entering the inner chamber of the building. This temple was destroyed by a fire, started deliberately by Herostratos, in 356BC. The visit of Alexander the Great to the city in 334BC traditionally inspired the rebuilding of the temple. Foundations of the temple can still be seen in situ and architectural fragments are also on display in the British Museum.

THE MAUSOLEUM AND COLOSSUS OF RHODES

Foundations of the 4th-century BC monumental tomb of Mausolus of Caria can still be seen at Bodrum, the site of the ancient city of Halikarnassos in western Turkey. The tomb was decorated with a series of reliefs showing the battle between the Amazons and the Greeks. These were later removed to construct the castle overlooking the harbour; they are now in the British Museum. The colossal statue of Helios (the sun) at Rhodes was built after the unsuccessful siege of the city by Demetrios Poliorcetes in 305–304BC. Ancient sources suggest that it stood to the equivalent of 33m (108ft). However no traces of it can be seen today.

LATER WONDERS

Later traditions adapted or added to the list. Pliny the Elder (who was killed in the eruption of Vesuvius in AD79) in his *Natural History* added the great Pharos (or lighthouse) in Alexandria in Egypt; underwater excavations have started to find remains of Ptolemaic Alexandria in the vicinity of the site. Among Pliny's additions was the labyrinth at Knossos on Crete, though by this time the Bronze Age palace was buried and the site occupied by a Roman settlement. Other writers added the sanctuary of Asklepios at Pergamom in western Turkey and the Capitol at Rome. By Late Antiquity the Christian basilica of Hagia Sophia in Constantinople was acknowledged as worth seeing.

Above: Marble frieze from the Mausolus of Caria, Bodrum, Turkey, depicting the Battle of the Greeks and Amazons (now in the British Museum)

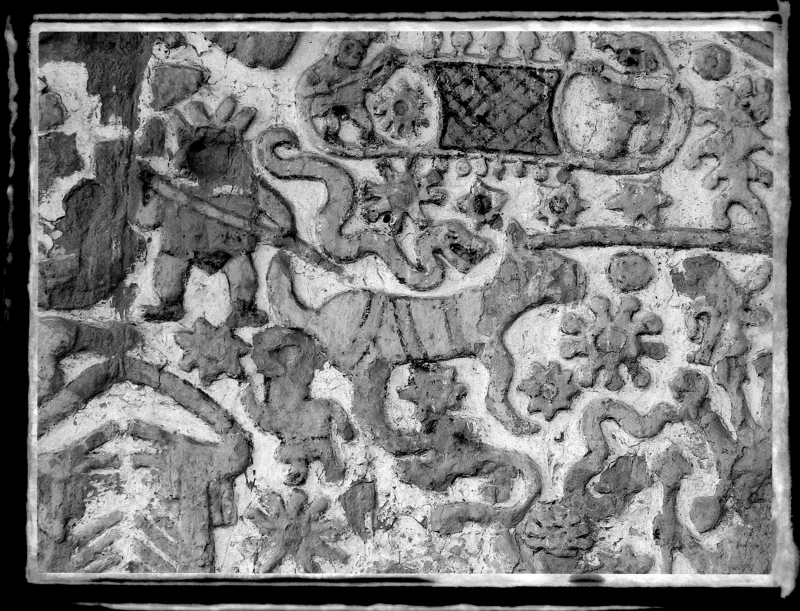

THE AMERICAS

HEAD-SMASHED-IN

IN THE FOOTHILLS OF SOUTHERN ALBERTA, HEAD-SMASHED-IN
IS ONE OF THE OLDEST AND BEST-PRESERVED BUFFALO JUMPS
IN THE WORLD. HERE OVER THE CENTURIES THOUSANDS OF
BISON WERE DRIVEN TO THEIR DEATH IN ORDER TO PROVIDE
PLAINS INDIANS WITH THEIR BASIC SUSTENANCE.

WHERE IS IT?
18km (11 miles) west of Fort
McLeod in southern Alberta,
Canada

WHEN TO VISIT
Open all year with the exception
of Christmas Eve, Christmas Day,
New Year's Day and Easter Sunday.
Summer and winter opening hours
differ slightly

GENERAL INFO
Designated a UNESCO World
Heritage Site in 1981, the site has a
state-of-the-art interpretive centre.
Online information can be found at
www.head-smashed-in.com

Situated on a sheer cliff at the eastern edge of the
foothills of southern Alberta, Head-Smashed-In buffalo
jump provides eloquent archaeological testimony to
5,500 years of hunting prowess by Plains Indians. So
successful were they that the site was used almost
continuously until the near extinction of the buffalo in
the late 19th century AD.

THE KILL
The site complex comprises four discrete elements—
gathering basin, drive lanes, kill site, processing and
camp site. The gathering basin was a well-watered
grassy area of approximately 40sq km (15.5sq miles).
Here small groups of bison would patiently and surrep-
titiously be herded into larger groups. When a sufficient
number of animals had been gathered they would be
driven in a controlled stampede down the drive lanes,
which comprised lines of stone cairns. Other members
of the tribe would stand here, making sure that the
animals kept to their pre-ordained path. The drive lanes
extend back as much as 14km (9 miles) from the cliff
edge. The kill site was located here; the buffalo were
driven over the edge and fell to their deaths below.
If they were not killed outright, hunters waited with
spears, bows and arrows or clubs to finish them off.

Today, close to 11m (36ft) of earth and stratified bone
deposits remain. After initial butchering, the carcasses
were transported to the processing and camp site. Here

tribal members processed the meat and skeletons,
efficiently utilizing nearly all of the carcasses. Meat
could be eaten fresh, or dried, or turned into pemmican
(a storable mixture of dried meat, bison grease and
berries). Bones were smashed open for marrow or
turned into household objects like scrapers, awls
or needles. Archaeologists have even excavated the
boiling pits used to render the bone down. The hide was
used for clothing or the construction of the tepee, the
common habitation structure of the Plains Indian.

Above: View of the Head-Smashed-In buffalo jump

WHAT'S IN A NAME?

The colourful name, Head-Smashed-In, was given to the site by the Blackfoot Indians, the tribe that occupied southern Alberta and adjacent Montana until they were forced into reservations in the 19th century. The name may refer either to the fact that it was here the buffalo had their heads smashed by the fall, or to an actual Blackfoot Indian whose own head was smashed in during the drive.

Below: Buffalo on the edge

L'Anse-aux-Meadows

WHERE IS IT?

At the northern end of the island of Newfoundland, Eastern Canada

WHEN TO VISIT

Open 1 June to 8 October 9–6. The park recommends calling a few days before your anticipated arrival to ensure that the site is open (tel. 709 623 2608)

GENERAL INFO

L'Anse-aux-Meadows was designated a UNESCO World Heritage site in 1978. One feature of the site is three reconstructed Norse buildings. Online information can be obtained at www.pc.gc.ca

L'ANSE-AUX-MEADOWS

THIS REMARKABLE SITE, FOUND IN 1960 BY THE HUSBAND-AND-WIFE TEAM OF HELGE AND ANNE STINE INGSTAD AND EXCAVATED BY THEM DURING THE FOLLOWING DECADE, PROVIDES INDISPUTABLE PROOF THAT EUROPEANS HAD SETTLED NORTH AMERICA LONG BEFORE CHRISTOPHER COLUMBUS.

Right: View of the Viking village of Norsted, at L'Anse-aux-Meadows, Newfoundland

Later excavations were conducted by Parks Canada, and the work revealed the remains of eight houses, the largest of which was approximately 29m x 15m (95ft x 49ft). These houses were probably made of turf on a wooden frame. Also recovered were smaller buildings, a smithy and a charcoal kiln, a carpentry workshop and typical Viking objects from the 11th century AD. These artefacts included such items as a bronze pin, a stone oil lamp, a bone needle and a whetstone.

SHORT LIVED

The inhabitants of the village also left behind garbage dumps, called middens by archaeologists. However, these were very shallow, suggesting that the period of occupation was quite short, perhaps as brief as 30 years. Why this was the case is unclear. It may simply have been because the climate was too harsh for agriculture to serve as the primary means of sustenance. Or the settlement may have been too remote from other Viking settlements for its inhabitants to feel safe, for it is documented that the Norse did not have peaceful relations with the local indigenous inhabitants whom they called Skraelings.

THE NAME

L'Anse aux Meadows could have been established by Erik the Red following his banishment from Norway in AD982, or by his son Leif Erikson. This part of North America is surely the area referred to by the Vikings as 'Vinland'. However, the exact derivation of this word is unclear – 'vin' might refer to grapes or wine, or to grass or pasture (even today the area surrounding L'Anse-aux-Meadows is meadow-like, hence its modern name). Either of these names might have been deployed to entice potential settlers to sign on.

IMPORTANT DISCOVERIES

The excavation of L'Anse-aux-Meadows is important not just for its archaeological and historical significance, but also because it demonstrates conclusively that it was not the Spanish, English or French who first colonized the so-called New World. And it is the descendants of these three nations who often, and as we now know incorrectly, proclaim themselves as having a special place in the hierarchy of Europeans in the New World.

Above: Part of the reconstructed settlement of L'Anse-aux-Meadows

Mesa Verde

MESA VERDE

THE ARCHAEOLOGICAL SITES SET ON THE MESAS OF SOUTHEASTERN COLORADO DOCUMENT THE ANCESTRAL PUEBLOAN WAY OF LIFE BETWEEN AD500 AND 1300. MESA VERDE IS A UNESCO WORLD HERITAGE SITE.

Mesa Verde is Spanish for 'green table' and this accurately describes the flat-topped series of mesas that make up the park. It was designated as a national park by President Theodore Roosevelt in 1906 in order to 'preserve the works of man'. Archaeologists have identified over 4,000 archaeological sites here. Most of these are found on the tops of the mesas with good access to water and arable land. Here, using dry-land techniques as well as irrigation systems, the Ancestral Puebloans grew such crops as maize, beans and squash.

ANCESTRAL PUEBLOANS' LIFESTYLE

At first they lived in semi-subterranean pithouses, which were roofed with timber beams and a lattice of smaller branches and mud (adobe). However, they later converted to above-ground dwellings around AD750, with the pit structures evolving into ceremonial/religious buildings called 'kivas'. At first the Ancestral Puebloans restricted themselves to simple coil-made grey pottery, but over time began to produce magnificently painted pottery of a variety of shapes and sizes.

NEW HABITATION

Towards the end of their occupation of the Mesa Verde, they made the remarkable decision to abandon the mesa tops and build very large and elaborate apartment complexes (the best way to describe them) in large rock overhangs on the sides of the mesa walls. There are about 600 of these, and the largest of them is called Cliff Palace. It has 150 rooms and 75 open areas. Twenty-one of the rooms appear to have been kivas, and there are up to 30 rooms that were used as residences. It is estimated that at any one time as many as 120 people were living there. Why the Ancestral Puebloans built these structures is still unclear. It may have been for defence against intruders, or possibly moving off the mesa tops may have opened up more land for growing crops (this period was wracked by a series of droughts). However, their occupation of the cliff dwellings was brief and, by the end of the 13th century, Mesa Verde, like the rest of the Four Corners region, had been abandoned for areas to the south and west, where the Ancestral Puebloans could still grow their traditional crops.

Right and next spread: Cliff Palace, the largest habitation at Mesa Verde

Left: Square Tower House ruin in Navajo Canyon, Mesa Verde

ORIGINS OF THE ANCESTRAL PUEBLOAN NAME

For many years the archaeological remains from this part of Colorado were placed into the so-called 'Anasazi Tradition' (which extends over the Four Corners region of the USA). The term, which comes from a Navajo word, is variously translated as 'Enemy Ancestors' or 'Ancient Ones'. However, the living descendants of this tradition are not actually Navajo, but rather the Puebloan groups of the Four Corners (for example, Acoma, Zuni and Hopi). As a result, the term Anasazi has gradually lost popularity and most archaeologists now refer to the Ancestral Puebloan tradition.

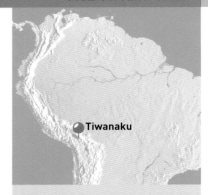

TIWANAKU

LOCATED IN THE HIGHLANDS OF BOLIVIA 15KM (9 MILES) SOUTHEAST OF LAKE TITICACA, AND MORE THAN 3,500M (11,480FT) ABOVE SEA LEVEL, THIS URBAN CENTRE WAS ONCE THE CAPITAL CITY OF A VAST AND POWERFUL TIWANAKU STATE, DATING TO 1000–400BC.

WHERE IS IT?

In the Titicaca basin, 72km (45 miles) from the Bolivian capital of La Paz, on the road towards Desaguadero, on the Peruvian border

WHEN TO VISIT

Any time of year, but if possible avoid the rainy season from December to March

GENERAL INFO

Weather in the highlands can be a bit misleading. While it is sunny and warm during the morning, it can be cold and windy during the afternoon

This archaic state extended its influence over the southern Andean region, reaching all the way to the coast of southern Peru and northern Chile. The capital city was sustained by high-altitude crops like potatoes from intensive farming around the shores of Lake Titicaca, and extensive llama caravans linked the metropolis to distant Tiwanaku colonies. The regional dispersal but discontinuous distribution of Tiwanaku's distinctive iconography and architecture caused scholars to question the nature of the political power held by the capital city. Based on the results of his current research in the periphery of the Tiwanaku state, Paul Goldstein has argued that, instead of holding a continuous control over its territory, the state was composed of a number of colonies spread all over the Southern Andes. Despite their location outside the heartland core, the settlers of these colonies kept their original cultural and religious identity and engaged in intensive trade with the capital city.

AKAPANA PYRAMID

The site of Tiwanaku is an urban centre composed of a monumental core with ceremonial buildings, monolithic gateways and great carved stones. The urban core is surrounded by 8–10sq km (3–4sq miles) of domestic structures that imply a very dynamic and densely populated area. Spanish conquistador Cieza de León visited the site in 1549, 500 years after its collapse, and recounted that the ruined megalopolis was dominated by a man-made hill of enormous size, erected upon massive stone foundations. This is the earliest account of the Akapana Pyramid, the largest structure at the city and the southernmost of great Andean platforms. The pyramid measures some 200m (656ft), and stands over 15m (49ft) high. The flat summit, surrounded by stone buildings, held a sunken court where ritual libations were performed. To the west of the pyramid there is another sunken court. The court walls were ornamented with numerous stone

Above: The Gateway of the Sun, an important icon to the people of Tiwanaku

Left: One of the impressive statues at Tiwanaku, representing a ruler or deity of the city

Left opposite: Part of the sunken court, with its ornamentation of stone heads

heads representing human skulls. It is believed a large collection of carved stone monoliths were once set in the court floor. The most famous of these stone works is the Bennett monolith, the largest known Andean stela. Decorated in Classic Tiwanaku style, the Bennett monolith depicts an elegantly garbed human figure, probably a ruler or a god, holding a libation vessel in one hand and a baton-like object in the other.

GATEWAY OF THE SUN

The best-known piece of Tiwanaku stonework is the Gateway of the Sun. The top of the portal is dominated by a central anthropomorphic figure known as the Gateway God. Resembling a sunburst, the Gateway God is thought by some scholars to be a solar god and the antecedent of later Andean deities. In this sense, Tiwanaku's rich and mysterious iconography has been interpreted by many experts as the centre of the highland state's ideology—an ideology that was spread all over the southern Andes by settlers from the Tiwanaku heartland.

COPÁN

WHILE PALENQUE DOMINATED THE WESTERN BOUNDARY OF THE CLASSIC MAYA REALM, COPÁN LAY AT THE EASTERN EXTREME, NEAR WHERE MESOAMERICA MEETS LOWER CENTRAL AMERICA.

Copán

WHERE IS IT?
In western Honduras, generally reached overland from Guatemala City, 250km (155 miles) to the west

WHEN TO VISIT
Winter months are recommended

GENERAL INFO
Visitors stay in the quaint town of Copán Ruinas, within walking distance of the archaeological site

Because of this setting, unusual both ethnically and geologically (rich in volcanic tuff rather than the typical limestone), Copán represents a distinct regional development of Classic Maya civilization. Using resilient volcanic stone, Copán produced the most admired three-dimensional sculpture and some of the most lushly decorated buildings of any Maya site.

THE COPÁN DYNASTY

A remarkable royal portrait gallery, Altar Q depicts all 16 kings who reigned between the 5th and early 9th centuries, even glyphically noting the arrival of the dynastic founder in AD426. This pivotal figure, K'inich Yax K'uk' Mo', seems to have been sent from a site in the Maya heartland, perhaps near Tikal, to colonize a

Right: Ballcourt at Copán

frontier in proximity to jade, obsidian and other lithic resources. Burials from this period, including that of the founder's wife, show direct ties to Teotihuacán. Yax K'uk' Mo' was lionized throughout Copán's history. One astonishing tribute is a sculpted stucco façade on the Margarita Structure that expands his hieroglyphic name, meaning Blue-Green Quetzal Macaw, into full-blown birds.

The artistic legacy of the 13th dynast reigning in the 8th century, Waxak Lajuun Ub'aah K'awiil, is noteworthy for nine stelae in the Main Plaza, baroque compositions of intricate symbols, considered the most splendid of all Maya stelae. He also commissioned some of the finest standing architecture, including the Hieroglyphic Stairway, the ballcourt and Structure 22 with its unique array of cosmic symbols in stone.

DISCOVERY OF EARLY CLASSIC SUBSTRUCTURES

The changing course of the Copán River over centuries has exposed early stratigraphic layers on the east face of the Acropolis. Successful tunnelling here, and later in Temples 16 and 26, revealed well-preserved Early Classic buildings and caches; several tunnels are open to the public. The most extraordinary find is a complete Early Classic building (dubbed Rosalila) from the sixth-century reign of Moon Jaguar, found within Temple 16. A full-scale replica recreating the carved and painted stucco can be seen in the site museum.

SITES AROUND THE COPÁN VALLEY

Many places of interest are scattered around the architectural centre, including the Sepulturas Group, a residential compound of craft specialists and high-ranking officials. Several stelae set around the Copán Valley by a seventh-century ruler can be visited on horseback, as can a rocky outcrop carved with large toads, known as Los Sapos.

Left: Stone portrait of Maya ruler Waxak Lajuun Ub'aah K'awiil

Chichén Itzá

WHERE IS IT?
120km (74.5 miles) east of Mérida and 150km (93 miles) west of Cancún in Mexico

WHEN TO VISIT
Yucatán is warm year-round, but winter months are optimal

GENERAL INFO
Included with the price of admission is a sound and light show, held every evening in the ruins

Above: Detail of a Maya wall carving

Right: The Pyramid of Kukulkan overshadows the Temple of a Thousand Columns

CHICHÉN ITZÁ

CHICHÉN ITZÁ IS AMONG ANCIENT AMERICA'S BEST-KNOWN CITIES. SPRAWLING OVER THE PLAINS OF NORTHERN YUCATÁN, MORE THAN A DOZEN ARCHITECTURAL COMPLEXES OFFER SPECTACULAR SIGHTSEEING.

The imposing edifices reflect an architectural explosion that began on the eve of the collapse of southern lowland Classic Maya kingdoms, when the centre of Maya culture shifted to the north and remained there until the Spanish conquest.

THE SACRED WELL OF THE ITZÁ

Because Northern Yucatán is bereft of surface water, its ancient inhabitants relied on water-filled sinkholes, called 'cenotes', during dry times. In the heart of the ancient city is one of the peninsula's largest cenotes; indeed, Chichén Itzá means 'mouth of the well of the Itzá'. Approached by a stone causeway, the Sacred Cenote was an important religious shrine. Material dredged from the bottom showed not just evidence of human sacrifice but also gold artefacts from as far away as Costa Rica and Colombia, in addition to rarely preserved wood, rubber and incense. The Itzá were a political faction that chronicles say took over Chichén Itzá, apparently amidst the ninth-century AD turmoil of the Maya collapse.

THE PUUC AND TOLTEC ART STYLES AT CHICHÉN ITZÁ

Much has been made of Chichén Itzá's divergent art styles. Buildings in the southern sector, or Old Chichén, reflect a centuries-old architectural formula known as the Puuc style. However, in the northern sector, or New Chichén, buildings dramatically break with the Classic Maya tradition, closely paralleling the site of Tula, the Toltec capital north of Mexico City. For instance, the reclining Chac Mools, which influenced the English sculptor Henry Moore, are found at both sites. It was long believed that Toltecs invaded Chichén Itzá and imposed their culture on the Maya. This assumption is now called into question; rather, scholars believe the Itzá Maya interacted with the Toltecs and together they forged a new international style strongly infused with central Mexican ideology, especially regarding the Feathered Serpent. Throughout the Early Postclassic period, until about AD1200, political power rested on militaristic cults dedicated to the Feathered Serpent, depictions of which abound at Chichén Itzá.

TOLTEC BUILDINGS

Chichén Itzá's most famous edifices are in the Toltec sector, dating between AD900 and 1000. El Castillo has gained international fame for its unique interaction of architecture with the setting equinox sun that casts a zigzag shadow meeting a carved serpent head at the base of the staircase. Thousands gather to witness this 'serpent' apparition in March—El Castillo was named one of the Seven Wonders of the World in a recent internet survey. Flanked by massive colonnaded halls bearing hundreds of reliefs originally painted in gaudy colours, the Temple of the Warriors was the principal centre of military cult rituals. The 140m (459ft) long Great Ballcourt is the largest in Mesoamerica. Rings for scoring points remain and temples replete with murals and carvings overlook the playing field. Just east is the Tzompantli, a platform for displaying human skulls, dozens of which are depicted on the walls.

LA VENTA

MESOAMERICA'S UNIQUE BLEND OF ART, CEREMONIAL
ARCHITECTURE, RELIGION, AND POLITICS FIRST APPEARS WITH
THE OLMEC, MESOAMERICA'S MOTHER CULTURE.

La Venta

WHERE IS IT?

El Parque-Museo La Venta
(La Venta Park-Museum) is in
Villahermosa, Tabasco (Mexico);
the archaeological ruins are 150km
(93 miles) northwest

WHEN TO VISIT

Winter months are best to visit this
humid, rainy area

GENERAL INFO

El Parque-Museo La Venta
features an outdoor installation of
La Venta's stone monuments

Settling the floodplains of Mexico's Gulf Coast, the
Olmec had a vibrant civilization between 1200 and
400BC that stimulated the formation of complex
societies from Mexico to El Salvador. The Olmec can
be credited with Mesoamerica's earliest expressions
of monumental architecture, sculpture, a pantheon of
gods, hieroglyphic writing and even the earliest known
use of rubber in the world.

LA VENTA'S RISE

Olmec sites were ruled by divine chiefs of
unprecedented power in Mesoamerica, much
of it derived from long-distance trade in such
exotic goods as jade, haematite and obsidian;
indeed, basalt was transported from 60km
(37 miles) away to produce massive stone
sculptures. San Lorenzo, Veracruz, was
the first Olmec site to exhibit such
heights of political centralization and
wealth, around 1200BC. However, it
mysteriously declined around
900BC just as La Venta rose
to prominence; La Venta
likewise declined around
400BC marking the end of
Olmec civilization.

**Right: An Olmec figure known as
'The Governor' complete with cape and
elaborate headdress**

Above: 16 male Olmec figurines, found buried in layers of coloured sand

BURIAL MOUNDS

The architectural core of La Venta is the best preserved of any Olmec ceremonial centre and shows a formalized plan with long earthen mounds in an axial alignment punctuated by a 33m (108ft) high pyramid, the earliest in Mesoamerica. An exceptional suite of burials and offerings was excavated beneath mounds and plaza floors. The La Venta Olmec buried stone monuments, figurines and tons of exotic stone, often in carefully arranged layers of coloured sands and clays.

MASTERPIECES OF LA VENTA

La Venta produced some of the Olmec's greatest artworks. Its four colossal heads, representations of chiefs standing up to 3m (10ft) high, follow a formula seen earlier at San Lorenzo. Seven so-called 'altars', really thrones, are found at La Venta. Icons of Mesoamerican art, Altars 4 and 5 show a ruler sitting in a cave exemplifying Mesoamerica's enduring connection between sacred landscape and kingship. The earliest Mesoamerican stelae, erect flat stones with figural depictions, later a mainstay of Maya art, occur at La Venta. Indeed, Mesoamerica's great tradition of relief sculpture begins at this Olmec site.

MONTE ALBÁN

BETWEEN 500BC AND AD750 THE ZAPOTEC LORDS OF MONTE ALBÁN CREATED ONE OF THE MAJOR STATE LEVEL SOCIETIES OF ANCIENT MESOAMERICA.

Monte Albán

WHERE IS IT?
9km (5.5 miles) from Oaxaca City, Mexico

WHEN TO VISIT
Any time of year, but expect more rain from July to October

GENERAL INFO
Visit the site museum where a collection of hieroglyphically inscribed stone monuments is housed. For more information go online at www.inah.gob.mx

Right: Looking southwest across Monte Albán, a UNESCO World Heritage Site

Far right: Mutilated captive engraved on stone

Oaxaca's largest and most powerful urban centre during the Classic period (AD150–750), Monte Albán fostered the development of Zapotec art and writing while carrying on bustling trade with Teotihuacán, a cosmopolitan city with its own Zapotec merchant district.

CLASSIC SPLENDOUR

Monte Albán was strategically situated on a 400m (1,312ft) eminence above the Valley of Oaxaca near the convergence of its main branches. Zapotecs transformed this overlook into an acropolis featuring a 300m (984ft) long plaza flanked on the east and west by a line of palaces and ceremonial buildings, including a ballcourt, and on the north and south by broad platforms supporting building groups. Construction spills down the mountainside, mainly residential complexes and elite tombs, some decorated with polychrome murals. Echoing the distant mountains, the Classic temples lining the plaza have wide staircases and a characteristic moulding in the form of an inverted U.

PRECLASSIC BEGINNINGS

While most of Monte Albán's standing architecture is Classic, a Preclassic platform underneath Building L is one of the site's oldest structures and was originally faced with hundreds of stone reliefs of nude, typically emasculated, bleeding captives. These so-called Danzantes not only preserve early Zapotec writing in the form of calendar dates, actually representing

names, but also testify to the military ethos of early Monte Albán. Another fascinating Preclassic construction is Building J; its unusual arrowhead shape probably marks an astronomical alignment. The walls are inscribed with place signs, among the earliest known in Mesoamerica, juxtaposed to an inverted head, thought to be a conquered chief, again reflecting Monte Albán's military posture. These place signs have been identified with sites in the surrounding region.

CLASSIC TOMBS AND DECLINE

Classic Monte Albán saw the consolidation of an elite class of noble families, evident in dozens of tombs scattered around the site; the famous Tombs 104 and 105 are still accessible to visitors by posted trails. These tombs contain brilliant frescoes featuring men and women in ritual scenes. The prestige of royal families and ancestors is also evident on Classic Zapotec bas-reliefs depicting married couples beseeching the gods. Tribute ensured Monte Albán's wealth, as did long-distance trade with Teotihuacán. The fall of Teotihuacán at the end of the Classic period may have precipitated Monte Albán's decline by AD800 and, shortly after, the intrusion of the Mixtecs, their linguistic cousins who rose to prominence during the Postclassic period. Mixtecs reused Tomb 7 at Monte Albán and left the largest cache of gold objects ever found in Mesoamerica. At the end of Classic times Monte Albán suffered slow and steady depopulation, as the focus of culture moved to other centres.

ZAPOTEC FUNERARY URNS

Gray-ware funerary urns with attached figures are found in tombs at Monte Albán and other Zapotec sites. Masterpieces of ceramic sculpture, they depict humans impersonating gods, such as the maize and rain gods.

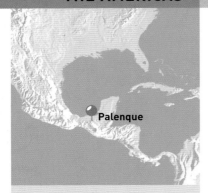

Palenque

PALENQUE

FLOWERING BETWEEN AD600 AND 800 AMIDST THE WATERFALLS AND RIVERS OF THE CHIAPAS HIGHLAND FOOTHILLS, PALENQUE IS HOME TO THE MOST FAMOUS TOMB OF THE ANCIENT AMERICAS, THAT OF THE RULER K'INICH JANAHB PAKAL I (HENCEFORTH PAKAL), DISCOVERED IN 1952 AT THE BASE OF A HIDDEN STAIRCASE IN THE TEMPLE OF THE INSCRIPTIONS.

WHERE IS IT?
The closest major city is Villahermosa, Tabasco, 140km 87 miles) northeast of Palenque (Mexico)

WHEN TO VISIT
November to February, the coolest driest months, are recommended

GENERAL INFO
Many of Palenque's long-admired treasures, as well as recently discovered sculptural masterpieces in ceramic, limestone and stucco, are on display in the site museum

OTHER FAMOUS BUILDINGS
The Temple of the Inscriptions and the Group of the Cross—three temples commemorating the accession of Pakal's son, Kan B'alam II, in AD684—are found south of the Palace. The world-renowned carved lid of Pakal's sarcophagus is now hoisted above his interment in the Temple of the Inscriptions. North of the Palace is Palenque's lone ballcourt.

Installed in AD615, Pakal engineered Palenque's political fortunes and initiated a sculptural and architectural programme that have made this site a gem among Classic Maya cities.

PALENQUE PALACE

Pakal's first ambitious architectural project, the Palace, is a boxy arrangement of corbel-vaulted buildings and plazas resting on a high platform networked by subterranean tunnels. These features, as well as the lofty Tower, are unique to Maya architecture. The Palace walls are encrusted with stucco sculpture, most spectacularly on the piers of House D. Pakal's limestone inaugural monument, the Oval Palace Tablet, remains mounted in House E. The Courtyard of the Captives, abutting House C, has an impressive display of captives on limestone panels.

RECENT DISCOVERIES

Since the 1990s a string of archaeological discoveries at Palenque have yielded new treasures, such as the cache of 100 ceramic incense burner stands found in the platform of the Temple of the Cross. The Temple of the Red Queen, near the Temple of the Inscriptions, revealed the burial of a woman strewn with red cinnabar and jade. Most significantly, carved limestone panels found in Temples 19 and 21 have refined our understanding of Palenque's dynastic history, particularly concerning the reign of K'inich Ahk'al Mo' Nahb' III, inaugurated in AD721, who commissioned some of the finest narrative reliefs from the Maya area. While several rulers succeeded him, Palenque went silent around AD800, ending a dynasty of some 20 rulers whose names are recorded in hieroglyphic texts, among the most detailed historical records known for any Classic Maya kingdom.

Left: An aerial view of the magnificent buildings at Palenque

Right: Detail of a Maya Classic period relief sculpture of a warrior king

TEOTIHUACÁN

THE MOST ARCHITECTURALLY IMPOSING CITY SURVIVING THE RAVAGES OF TIME AND COLONIAL CONQUEST IN MEXICO, TEOTIHUACÁN WAS THE GREAT POWER OF CLASSIC MESOAMERICA AND EXERTED INFLUENCE AS FAR AWAY AS CENTRAL AMERICA.

WHERE IS IT?
40km (25 miles) northeast of Mexico City

WHEN TO VISIT
Any time of year, but expect summer rain and heat

GENERAL INFO
The scale of the site means hiking is essential, so dress appropriately. Masterpieces recovered from Teotihuacán can be viewed at Mexico City's National Museum of Anthropology, as well as the site museum south of the Pyramid of the Sun

Teotihuacán's impact on Mesoamerican history was profound. Indeed, the collapse of the Classic Maya kingdoms and rise of Early Postclassic states, such as the Toltecs, may be linked to Teotihuacán's violent fall around AD600.

ORIGINS AND LAYOUT OF THE CITY

At the beginning of the first millennium Teotihuacán coalesced rapidly as people throughout the Valley of Mexico began to relocate here, possibly fleeing drought or volcanic activity. By AD100 a precisely organized urban plan was implemented whereby the entire city, from temples to dwellings, followed an exacting grid.

Today a visitor can see 19sq km (7sq miles) of densely packed construction, but the city was originally much larger and had at its height a population of 200,000. The Street of the Dead, a 4km (2.5-mile) long processional way defining the north–south axis, is punctuated by the mammoth Pyramids of the Sun and Moon. The largest pyramid in Mesoamerica, measuring 200m (656ft) per side and 65m (213ft) tall, the Pyramid of the Sun is built over a sacred cave. Further south, the Ciudadela (Citadel), an enormous enclosure housing royal palaces and the ornate Temple of the Feathered Serpent, was the seat of political administration. City dwellers lived in one of the 2,000 apartment compounds surrounding the ritual centre, and foreigners had their own neighbourhoods.

ECONOMIC BASE

Much like the Aztecs, Teotihuacán revelled in a military culture, although actual conquests remain a mystery. Far clearer is how the city accrued wealth and power economically from trade in obsidian. Four hundred obsidian workshops have been found at Teotihuacán, and its highly prized green obsidian turns up at sites across Mesoamerica. Teotihuacán established trading outposts in Guatemala to further its economic ambitions, and had interactions with Maya royalty that are only beginning to be understood.

ARTISTIC LEGACY

Teotihuacán made notable achievements in art and architecture. Terraced buildings bear a distinct *talud-tablero* (sloping base and panel) profile, and columns were used to construct large interior spaces. The most prolific form of public art is fresco painting, which originally covered most buildings. Today, portions of painted murals are preserved in apartment compounds, such as Tetitla and Tepantitla. Rich in symbolic detail, the imagery features ritual performers and supernaturals.

RECENT DISCOVERIES

In the 1980s Rubén Cabrera Castro and Saburo Sugiyama unearthed 200 human sacrifices from pits underneath the Temple of the Feathered Serpent. Most were young men dressed as warriors, proof of Teotihuacán's endemic militarism; yet bone chemistry revealed that they were, mysteriously, of Teotihuacán origin. Sugiyama's ongoing excavations at the Pyramid of the Moon have revealed seven stages of enlargement, the last as late as AD400. Remarkable burials contained the skeletons of caged, sacrificed animals, and one contained individuals possibly of Maya ethnicity.

Left: Intricate murals are a highlight of Teotihuacán

Next spread: The Pyramid of the Moon, Teotihuacán

Chan Chan

CHAN CHAN

CHAN CHAN WAS A VAST AND MAJESTIC URBAN CENTRE OF THE CHIMÚ EMPIRE, DATING TO AD900–1460, AND IS RECOGNIZED AS THE BIGGEST ANCIENT ADOBE (MUD BRICK) CITY OF THE WORLD.

WHERE IS IT?

On the north coast of Peru, 5km (3 miles) west of the city of Trujillo

GENERAL INFO

Open all year, tickets can be bought at the Site Museum of Chan Chan, where a guide can also be hired

PRESERVING CHAN CHAN

Currently the Peruvian state is sponsoring a long-term project devoted to the study and reconstruction of many unstudied areas. This project also focuses on the preservation of the areas that are visited by thousands of tourists every year.

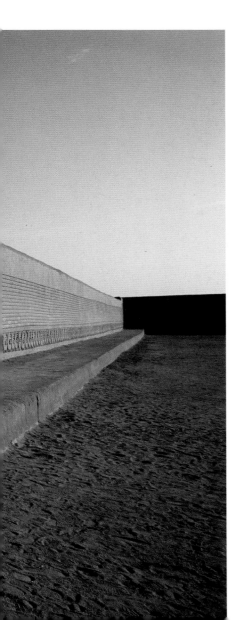

Close to the shore of the Pacific Ocean, this ancient city lived in close relation to the sea. Maritime themes and sea creatures were the most common motifs of the adobe friezes that graced the most important buildings of the city. This ancient metropolis was once the capital of the Chimú Empire, a powerful polity that flourished between AD900 and 1460. At the height of its reign the Chimú Empire extended its power over more than 500km (310 miles) of the South American Pacific coast, until it was defeated by the Inka army in 1460.

HIERARCHICAL HOUSING

The monumental constructions at the city of Chan Chan began about AD900, coinciding with the initial political consolidation of the region. At its apex Chan Chan was populated by more than 30,000 people, comprising rulers, nobles, craftsmen and servants. Its northern city wall enclosed an area of 20sq km (8sq miles), much of which was left empty, apparently set aside for further urban growth. The Chimú rulers and lords who lived at the heart of the city may have numbered 6,000 or less, and lived and worked in architecturally elaborate adobe compounds. The lesser nobility lived in 30 small compounds with low walls, while paramount rulers held court in palatial structures called 'ciudadelas' (citadels).

CIVIC GRANDEUR

The densely packed civic centre of great enclosures and other buildings covered an area of 6sq km (2sq miles). This was the area of the site where state decisions were made. The most representative structures located within the ciudadelas are small u-shaped buildings called 'audiencias' (reception courts). Measuring just about 4sq m (43sq ft), the audiencias have beautiful interior wall niches and gabled roofs. Iconographic depictions show richly garbed figures standing in the centre of these buildings in front of an assembled audience. According to archaeologist Michael Moseley, these special buildings were the offices of the Chimú kings and ruling nobility.

HOUSING THE WORKERS

Another 3,000 people lived immediately adjacent to the royal enclosures, which they served directly. It is estimated that some 26,000 craftsmen and women lived in densely occupied neighbourhoods surrounding the ciudadelas along the southern and western margins of the city. In these areas, different types of architecture and construction materials distinguish class and occupation. The lower class metropolitan majority lived and worked in quarters comprising small patios and irregular rooms of cane construction. Evidence recovered from these structures indicates that they were occupied by technicians and craftsmen. There was wood and lapidary work, but the dominant concern was large-scale metallurgical production and weaving.

HUACA DE LA LUNA

HUACA DE LA LUNA IS A CIVIC CEREMONIAL COMPLEX OF THE MOCHE CULTURE, AD500–800, LOCATED IN THE HEARTLAND OF THE MOCHE POLITY. IT IS A COMPLEX OF TWO IMPOSING ADOBE (MUD BRICK) MONUMENTAL PLATFORMS SEPARATED BY A BUSTLING URBAN ZONE.

WHERE IS IT?
On the northern coast of Peru, 4km (2.5 miles) from the city of Trujillo, near the mouth of the Moche River

GENERAL INFO
Tickets can be bought at the Site Museum where guides are also available all year round

The northern platform, Huaca del Sol, was largely destroyed by looters during the colonial period, but the southern platform, Huaca de la Luna did not suffer considerable damage. The southern platform was built near the uphill side of a prominent rock outcrop, Cerro Blanco, leaving a high vertical stony face exposed to viewers below.

SACRIFICIAL EVIDENCE
Scholars argue that this southern platform was the ceremonial stage for gruesome human sacrifices depicted in Moche iconography. In fact, one of the recurrent themes in Moche iconography involves the mountain-top sacrifice of captive warriors. Excavations conducted by Santiago Uceda and Steve Bourget in a patio built around a natural rock outcrop uncovered more than a dozen corpses of mature males killed by blows to the head, slit throats and other violent acts. Some of the corpses excavated show evidence of being deposited in muddy ground. This fact has led archaeologists to the conclusion that some sacrifices took place during moments of climatic stress caused by the torrential El Niño rainfall.

POLYCHROME MURALS
Research at the large central platform of the Huaca de la Luna complex revealed that it grew through multiple stages of use and construction. Spacious summit

Right: Colourful figure found at the Huaca de la Luna complex

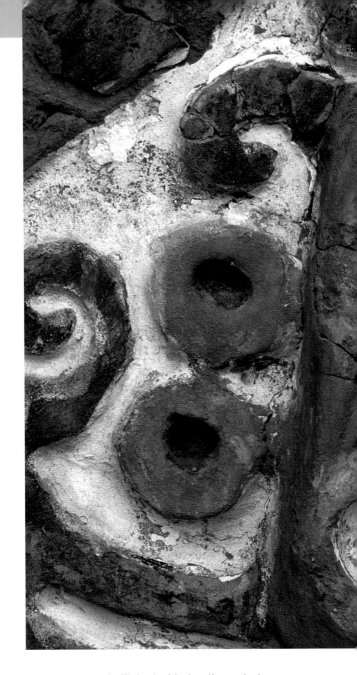

courts were embellished with dazzling polychrome murals. The murals show themes and characters common in Moche iconography. The forward-facing head of a large supernatural being with marked canine teeth, called 'Ai-apaec', was a common motif, while other panels depicted spider-like creatures,

anthropomorphic beings and parading captive warriors.

RULE AND RITUAL

Archaeologists have suggested that these richly ornamented courts were the sacrosanct settings for elaborate rituals that placated deities and maintained the social and cosmic order. In fact, experts in the subject believe that fine arts in the Moche polity were fully in the service of the political order and expressed a brilliant, often realistic, iconography that materialized an ideology of rule and ritual.

MOCHE SOCIETY

Currently, research at the Huaca de la Luna complex is focused on the study of the area in-between the two platforms. Excavations conducted by Santiago Uceda have revealed that, instead of the empty space once expected in Andean ceremonial centres, this was a heavily populated area. Elite and middle-class neighbourhoods have been identified as well as spaces for specialized craft production. All these findings portray the Moche as a heavily stratified society in which religious and political power were intertwined during the performance of rituals.

MACHU PICCHU

LOCATED ON A MOUNTAIN RIDGE AT 2,400M (7,874FT) ABOVE SEA LEVEL, MACHU PICCHU, A ROYAL COUNTRY ESTATE OF THE INKA EMPIRE, DATING TO AD1450–1530, IS THE MOST VISITED ARCHAEOLOGICAL SITE IN PERU.

WHERE IS IT?

In the Central Andean Highlands, 80km (50 miles) east of the city of Cuzco, Peru. You can take the tourist train from Cuzco to the nearby town of Aguas Calientes or the Inka Trail hike, which takes two to four days

WHEN TO VISIT

Avoid the rainy season from December to March

GENERAL INFO

Given the growing number of visitors and the Peruvian government's new regulations about the maximum number of people that can visit the site per day, plan the trip to Machu Picchu in advance through a tourist agency

Machu Picchu is also known as 'The lost city of the Inkas', and it remained unknown until it was discovered by the American archaeologist Hiram Bingham in 1911. Currently Machu Picchu is recognized as the most famous symbol of the Inka Empire. This breathtaking site was elected as a World Heritage Site by UNESCO in 1983 and formally announced in Lisbon in July 2007 as one of the New Wonders of the World after a worldwide online vote.

IMPOSING SPLENDOUR

Placed in a saddle between two mountains, with a commanding view down two valleys and a nearly impassable mountain at its back, Machu Picchu was built in the classical Inka Imperial style. Buildings were made out of beautifully polished drystone walls. The site is composed of 140 structures, including temples, residences and gardens. Temples and houses were distributed along paved streets surrounded by terraced gardens. All of these buildings were constructed and organized around aesthetic rather than functional priorities. For example, there are more than a hundred flights of stone steps at the site, most of them completely carved from a single block of granite. There are also a great number of water fountains, interconnected by channels and water-drainages perforated in the rock that were part of the original irrigation system. Evidence has been found to suggest that the irrigation system was used to carry water from a holy spring to each of the houses in turn.

DISTINCT DISTRICTS

The most impressive buildings at the site are located in a sector designated by archaeologists as the Sacred District. Here stands the Intihuatana or solar clock, a large carved and polished stone that projects the shadow of the sun in a different manner depending on the time of day. There is also the Temple of the Sun and the Room of Three Windows, which offers an amazing view of the valley below. It is believed that these structures were dedicated to Inti, the sun god and greatest deity of the Inka Empire. The Royal District of the site is where nobility lived. This sector of the site is composed of a number of multi-room household compounds characterized by typical Inka trapezoid-shaped rooms. The Popular District, or Residential District, is the area where it is believed the retainers lived. Located at the margins of the site, it includes storage buildings and simple domestic structures.

Above: Detail of the multi-room compounds that make up the Royal District

Previous page: Perched on a mountain ridge, the impressive ruins of Machu Picchu

INTELLECTUAL CONTROVERSY

For many years the nature and function of Machu Picchu remained a point of controversy among scholars. Based on its isolated location on a mountain ridge and its restricted access, the site was interpreted as a defensive outpost of the Inka Empire. Recent research conducted by Richard Burger and Lucy Salazar, based on materials recovered from Machu Picchu, is pointing towards an interesting new scenario. According to Burger and Salazar, instead of a defensive outpost, Machu Picchu was the royal country estate of one of the most powerful Inka emperors, Pachacuti. Burger and Salazar argue, based on their new historical, laboratory and field research, that the characteristics of the site suggest Machu Picchu was a royal estate where members of the Inka nobility retreated from the capital for rest, relaxation and other elite activities.

Below: Detail of stonework in the ruined buildings

Nasca

NAZCA

THE NAZCA CULTURE OCCUPIED THE ARID SOUTHERN COAST OF PERU BETWEEN 200BC AND AD800 AND IS FAMOUS FOR ITS DESERT MARKINGS AND GROUND DRAWINGS.

WHERE IS IT?

On the southern coast of Peru, 120km (74.5 miles) from the city of Ica, and 20km (12.5 miles) north of the city of Nazca

GENERAL INFO

The most popular way to visit the Nazca lines is to fly over the plateau. The flight takes around 30 minutes, and while there are about 20 companies that provide this service, it is best to make a reservation a day before during the high tourist season, from June to August

Although the nature of the Nazca political organization is still not fully understood, researchers are currently thinking of it as a confederacy of politically independent groups that shared the ceremonial site of Cahuachi. Despite its particularly beautiful polychrome ceramic tradition, the Nazca culture is best known for its markings and drawings that occupy the plateau flats between the rivers that defined Nazca territory.

NAZCA GLYPHS

The great concentration of figures on the Nazca plateau are by far the largest cultural artefacts of the region's ancient inhabitants. Called 'geoglyphs', the markings were created by brushing away and removing the upper, dark, oxidized desert sediments to expose lower, lighter-coloured surfaces. Experiments performed by archaeoastronomer Anthony Aveni and a small team of co-workers indicate that 16,000sq m (172,220sq ft) of desert pavement can be cleared in about a week's time. Therefore, very large figures could have been created by relatively small crews in a comparatively short period of time. Cleared sections of the desert are discernible at ground level, but very large compositions and long, flat lines cannot be seen in their integrity from the ground. It was only in the 1970s that the study of aerial photographs by Paul Kosok and Maria Reiche first discovered the exceptional concentration of glyphs on the 200sq km (77sq mile) Nazca plateau.

TYPES OF DESIGN

There are two dominant forms in the glyph designs. One is composed of lines and geometric designs, mostly triangles, trapezoids, zigzags, and spirals. Together the linear and geometric figures cover a staggering 3,600,000sq m (38,750,078sq ft), or about two per cent of the plateau surface. The second form's dominant motifs were taken from the natural world. There are about three dozen animal drawings,

Left: One of the Nazca figures, depicting a hummingbird

comprising birds, several killer whales, a monkey, a spider, a probable fox or llama, at least one human and a few plants.

UNDERSTANDING THE GLYPHS

Geoglyphs at Nazca and elsewhere certainly served more than one function. The calendrical significance of the lines has been suspected, but not yet demonstrated. Anthony Aveni and a team of anthropologists conducted the most systematic and extensive study yet of plateau geoglyphs and failed to find either statistically significant celestial correlations or directional correlations. However, lines were often found to radiate out from hills or high vantage points called 'ray centres'. Sixty-two such nodes were mapped and shown to be interconnected by long, linear geoglyphs thought to be trans-plateau pathways leading from one irrigated oasis to another Actually, glyphs are most numerous near irrigated, settled land, where younger designs cross older ones, indicating that the creations were used briefly and then abandoned.

THE ROLE OF GLYPHS

Although all geoglyphs are technically similar, each seems to have been created separately, used for a time and then forgotten. They are numerous and impressive, but do not represent great expenditures of energy. New figures cross old ones in amazing profusion, and the works were obviously not part of a larger, centralized conception planned by one mind at one time. Scholars believe that the Nazca lines represent the beliefs of the different groups within Nazca society; while everyone agreed that geoglyphs were important, each group created its own.

Above: Aerial view of Nazca's monkey geoglyph

EUROPE

Carnac Monuments

CARNAC MONUMENTS

ALONG THE GULF OF MORBIHAN IN SOUTHERN BRITTANY, A REGION OF ABOUT 300SQ KM (116SQ MILES) CONTAINS AN EXCEPTIONAL CONCENTRATION OF MEGALITHIC MONUMENTS.

WHERE IS IT?
On the southern coast of Brittany, France, along the Gulf of Morbihan

WHEN TO VISIT
Mainland sites at Carnac and Locmariaquer are open year-round; the island of Gavrinis is accessible by ferry between April and November

GENERAL INFO
There are visitor centres at Locmariaquer and Carnac. Carnac alignments open only for guided tours in the summer but can be seen from outside the fence. See www.ot-carnac.fr and www.france-for-visitors.com/brittany/south/locmariaquer.html for current information on times and fees

These monuments include long mounds, passage graves, upright stones known as 'menhirs' and alignments that are long rows of standing stones. At the centre of this megalithic paradise is the small resort of Carnac, whose archaeological reputation lies in the remarkable parallel rows of standing megalithic stones found just outside the town.

ER-GRAH MOUND
The Neolithic inhabitants of the coastal areas around the Gulf of Morbihan began to erect the monuments that define important locations in the landscape before 4000BC. Some of the earliest examples are found to the east of Carnac on the Locmariaquer peninsula, where a complex of sites includes the Er-Grah mound, the Grand Menhir Brisé and the Table des Marchands passage grave. The gigantic mound of Er-Grah was almost 200m (656ft) long in its original state. It is an outstanding example of a type of monument known as 'Carnac mounds', found along the Gulf of Morbihan, which had small burial chambers, many of which contain abundant grave goods.

GRAND MENHIR BRISÉ
Right next to the Er-Grah long mound is the Grand Menhir Brisé. Today, this massive granite pillar lies on its side, broken into four pieces. During the Neolithic, however, it stood over 20m (66ft) tall and weighed over 350 tons, the largest individual standing stone known from prehistoric Europe. It parallels a number of other colossal menhirs in the Morbihan region, although none quite so large as the Grand Menhir Brisé. Archaeologists have discovered empty footings in the vicinity of the Grand Menhir Brisé that are interpreted as locations where other such stones had once been erected and subsequently removed.

PASSAGE GRAVES
There is evidence that many of the menhirs were reused during the 4th millennium BC in the construction of another type of monument, the passage graves of the Atlantic fringe of northwestern Europe. An important example of such reuse of broken menhirs lies in two passage graves, La Table des Marchands and Gavrinis.

Left: Engraved stones in the passage of Gavrinis

La Table des Marchands is found next to the Er-Grah long mound and the fragments of the Grand Menhir Brisé, while Gavrinis is just offshore on an island of the same name. Gavrinis is one of the most spectacular examples of megalithic architecture in Brittany, with a passage 14m (46ft) long leading to a chamber about 2.5m (8ft) square. Almost all of the upright stones, as well as the roof and floor, are abundantly decorated with carved designs. Archaeologists were able to match horns carved on the roof slab of Gavrinis with an animal head carved on the roof of La Table des Marchands, and the broken edges of each stone matched as well. They were probably pieces of a single menhir that was pulled down, broken and reused.

ALIGNMENTS

The famous alignments of multiple parallel rows of standing stones are found on the outskirts of Carnac itself: Le Menec, Kermario and Kerlescan. They were built over several centuries, beginning just before 3000BC and ending around 2500BC. At Le Menec, 1,099 stones in 11 rows stretch for 1,167m (3,829ft) from west to east and are 100m (328ft) across at their widest point, while at Kermario 1,029 surviving stones in seven rows cover an area 100m (328ft) by 1,120m (3,674ft). The Kerlescan alignment is shorter and wider, about 880m (2,887ft) by 139m (456ft), with 594 stones in 13 rows.

 MYSTERIOUS MEANINGS

Archaeologists debate the purpose of the Carnac alignments. The theory that they marked processional paths leading to stone enclosures where rituals occurred has gained favour, while the suggestion that they formed a lunar observatory is viewed sceptically.

Above: The alignments of Le Menec

Pech Merle

WHERE IS IT?

Close to Cabrerets, in the Quercy region of southern France

WHEN TO VISIT

Primarily from 1 April to the end of October, but also open at other times, except from mid-December to mid-January

GENERAL INFO

Although Ice Age decorated sites continue to be found every year, many of those that used to be open to the public have had to be closed because of the risk of deterioration. So to visit those which remain open is a great privilege. Several excellent facsimiles already exist, and they will become more dominant in the future. The fine museum at the site provides an introduction to the prehistory of the region as well as to the cave's art

PECH MERLE

THE DECORATED ICE AGE CAVES OF EUROPE CONTAIN SOME OF THE GREATEST WORKS OF ART EVER PRODUCED, AND ABOUT 50 OF THEM CAN STILL BE VISITED, PRIMARILY IN FRANCE AND SPAIN, BUT ALSO IN ENGLAND, PORTUGAL AND ITALY.

Top right: Cave painting depicting mammoth and cattle from the Chapel of the Mammoths

Right: The Spotted Horse panel, which is considered a work of outstanding artistry

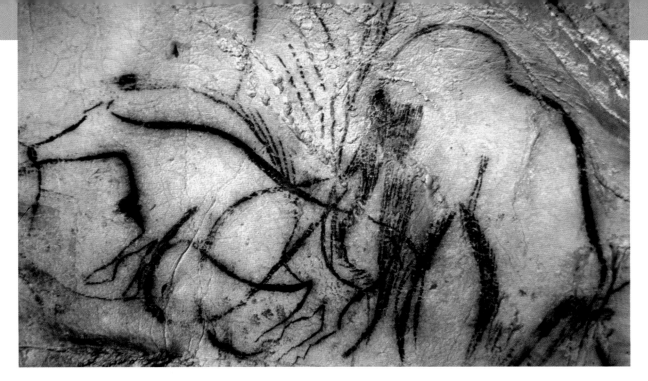

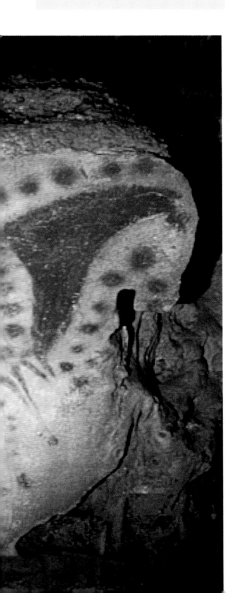

CAVE FORMATIONS

One major chamber in the cave contains huge natural stalagmitic discs that have fallen from the ceiling; there are also enormous formations that closely resemble the shaggy mammoths of the Black Frieze, and which may well have inspired the cave's artists.

Of all the decorated caves open to the public, Pech Merle (Blackbird Hill) is one of the most stunning, beautiful both for its stalagmitic formations and for its famous images. It was decorated at different periods between about 25,000 and 12,000 years ago. Although the cave was known throughout history, its wealth of Ice Age art was first discovered in 1922.

EARLY CAVE ART

The earliest phase comprises dots, circles and hand stencils, as well as simple finger meanders on the ceiling. The masterpiece of the phase is the famous Spotted Horse panel, 4m (13ft) in length, featuring two horses, back to back and partly superimposed, and a long red pike, six black hand stencils (all of the same hand, alternating palm-up and palm-down), seven red stencils of what may be bent thumbs, a red circle, and 28 red dots and 224 black dots placed in and around the horses. The right-hand horse uses the rock's shape, which naturally resembles a horse-head, although the two animals have stylized, very tiny heads. The horses, hands and dots were all made by spitting pigment. A radiocarbon date of 24,460 years ago was obtained from charcoal in the paint of the right-hand horse.

DEVELOPING CAVE ART

The second phase includes figures made with finger-tracings on the ceiling (mammoths, an ibex and some women bending forwards), as well as the cave's 40 black outline drawings, 24 of which are grouped on the famous 7m (23ft) 'Black Frieze' or 'Chapel of the Mammoths' (11 mammoths, five buffalo, four horses, four aurochs). Analysis has shown that this whole frieze was probably done in a spiralling composition by a single artist and experimentation suggests that it could have been done in an hour.

FLEETING VISITS

The final phase consists of some engravings, which include a bear's head. Pech Merle was never inhabited by Ice Age people, and the scant traces they left behind (just a few bones and flints and a dozen footprints of a young adolescent) suggest a series of rapid visits.

WHERE IS IT?

Towards the south of the island of Thera (also known as Santorini), Greece; there are buses to the site from Fira (the main town on the island) and the beach resort of Perissa

WHEN TO VISIT

The site has been closed for restoration since 2005; reopening date not confirmed

GENERAL INFO

Some of the finds from the early excavations at Akrotiri, including some of the best-known wall paintings, are on display at the National Archaeological Museum in Athens

AKROTIRI

THE ISLAND OF THERA, ALSO KNOWN AS SANTORINI, LIES IN THE AEGEAN SEA ABOUT 100KM (62 MILES) NORTH OF CRETE. A MAJOR VOLCANIC ERUPTION IN 1600–1500BC DESTROYED MUCH OF THE ISLAND AND BURIED THE TOWN OF AKROTIRI IN A BLANKET OF VOLCANIC ASH 20M (65FT) DEEP.

Right: One among many of the vibrant wall paintings discovered at Akrotiri

The excavations begun in 1967 by Spyridon Marinatos revealed remarkable preservation of the buildings, some still standing up to two storeys in height, and their contents. Many of the rooms were decorated with brightly coloured wall paintings, which have shed light on the appearance and activities of the people of Akrotiri.

Above: Amphorae are among everyday items found at Akrotiri that help to piece together life before the eruption

Right: A wall painting dating from around 1600BC portrays a fisherman

HIDDEN BY THE ERUPTION

The circumstances of the destruction of Akrotiri have enabled archaeologists to retrieve evidence that would not normally have survived, such as indication of the use of wooden furniture. Where cavities in the ash were located, plaster of Paris was poured in to reveal the shapes of tables and beds, their form preserved even though the wood from which they were made had rotted.

THE WALL PAINTINGS

Wall paintings were found in private houses and public buildings. In private houses, they were found in first-floor rooms only, as the ground floor was occupied primarily with the storage and preparation of food. In public buildings, both storeys had decorated walls. The particular importance of the wall paintings from Akrotiri is that they tend to be better preserved than at other Aegean sites, and the fragments are preserved within the rooms they actually decorated.

WHEN WAS AKROTIRI DESTROYED?

The latest scientific studies, published in 2006, suggest that the huge volcanic eruption that destroyed Akrotiri, which is conventionally dated to around 1500BC, occurred approximately a century earlier. Radiocarbon dating of an olive branch, which was buried alive when the volcano exploded, indicates the tree died between 1627 and 1600BC. These dates are supported by a separate project, which undertook radiocarbon dating of over 100 objects buried in the eruption. These findings are also roughly in line with earlier scientific studies. The debate continues, as it has been observed that these dates do not tally with correlations from ancient Egypt.

Left and right: Superbly preserved wall paintings depicting inhabitants of Akrotiri engaging in boxing

Athens

ATHENS

THE ARCHAEOLOGICAL PARK IN THE HEART OF ATHENS INCLUDES THE ACROPOLIS. THE PARTHENON IS ONE OF THE BEST-KNOWN TEMPLES OF THE ANCIENT GREEK WORLD.

WHERE IS IT?

The ancient Agora is in the Plaka district, which now forms a large archaeological park

GENERAL INFO

The archaeological site is open year-round. Useful metro stations are: Akropoli (Acropolis and theatre), Monastiraki (Agora) and Thiseio (Agora and Kerameikos). For further information go online at www.culture.gr

During the fifth century BC the city of Athens was transformed by the statesman Pericles. Among the greatest achievements was the refurbishment of the main sanctuary of the city on the Acropolis. His other work included connecting the ancient city with its harbour at Piraeus by a series of parallel defensive walls, and the refurbishment of the sanctuary of Demeter and Kore at Eleusis.

PERSIAN DESTRUCTION

Until the Persian destruction of the city in the autumn of 480BC, the Acropolis was protected by a series of

late Bronze Age (Mycenaean) walls. The Athenians had been building a new temple to their patron deity Athena. Remains of column drums and other architectural members can be clearly seen built into the north wall of the Acropolis, probably as a reminder of the impiety of the Barbarian invaders. Some of the archaic sculptures (korai and kouroi) were buried during the Athenian clean-up of the sanctuary and these can be seen in the Acropolis Museum.

THE ACROPOLIS

The Acropolis is approached through the monumental gateway or propylaia; surviving building accounts show that it was one of the last projects on the Acropolis before the outbreak of the Peloponnesian War (in 431BC). The north wing (on the left as you approach the gateway) contained a large dining hall; the south wing of the propylaia gave access to a separate sanctuary of Athena Nike (Victory) dominated by a small Ionic temple built in the 420s. The steps for a separate entrance can be seen in the side of the bastion.

THE PARTHENON

The Parthenon was designed to replace the earlier Temple of Athena (whose foundations can be made

Left: The Theseion (Temple of Hephaistos) at night from Areopagos hill in Athens

Right: The columns of the Doric temple of the Parthenon showing the relief sculptures

The statue of Athena Parthenos (Athena the virgin) was the most renowned cult image of Athens, made by the acclaimed sculptor Pheidias. There is a detailed description given by the ancient historian and Roman travel writer Pausanias. It stood in the Parthenon until the fifth century BC, when it may have been lost in a fire. A number of small-scale Roman marble copies inspired by the statue have been recovered.

out to its north). This contained the monumental gold and ivory statue of Athena Parthenos. The marble temple was decorated with three types of architectural sculptures (many of which are currently in London). The two triangular pediments at each end showed the battle between Poseidon and Athena for the control of Athens (west) and the birth of Athena (east). The square panels (metopes) were decorated with mythological scenes such as the battle between the Lapiths and Centaurs. On the outside of the inner building, but partly obscured by the columns, was the continuous frieze. This was in two parts, both starting at the southwest corner and meeting at the centre of the east end. It was decorated with riders, charioteers and animals being led to sacrifice; the east frieze showed the Olympian gods.

Although the temple was constructed in the 440s and early 430s it was in use for centuries afterwards, becoming a Christian church and even a mosque. At the east end traces of the shields mounted by Alexander the Great can be made out, as well as the holes for a monumental bronze inscription placed there by the Roman emperor Nero.

THE ERECHTHEION

To the north of the Parthenon lies the Erechtheion, which contains a number of different cult places including the marks where traditionally Poseidon's trident cut the ground. One of the most famous elements is the Caryatid porch, which contains six statues of women acting as columns; each holds a *phiale*, or libation dish, in her hand. (One of the statues is in London.) The porch was deliberately placed to overlap with the older Temple of Athena whose foundations can be seen. On the north side of the Erechtheion, architectural elements from the old temple can be viewed, built into the later walls.

THEATRE OF DIONYSOS

Athens was well known for its drama and the plays were performed in the Theatre of Dionysos on the south

Previous spread: The Parthenon from the Mouseion Hill

side of the Acropolis. The foundations of the temple to the god can be traced in the sanctuary surrounding the theatre. There is a semicircular orchestra (with a Roman period mosaic) for which the tiered seats are cut into the slope of the Acropolis. At the top of the slope can be seen some of the monuments erected by the victors in the dramatic competitions.

A later Roman concert hall (the Odeion) was given to the city by Herodes Atticus. This continues to be used for concerts and plays in the summer season.

ATHENIAN AGORA

Athens continues to be known as the birthplace of democracy. The public buildings, including the council chamber and law courts, were located in the agora that lies to the northwest of the Acropolis. The political buildings were constructed along the west edge of the open space, cut into a small hill on which the mid-fifth-century BC Temple of Hephaistos (popularly known as

Left: A section of the Porch of the Caryatids at the Erechtheion in the Acropolis, with six maidens supporting the roof

Below: Some of the seats reserved for dignitaries in the front row of the auditorium of the Theatre of Dionysos

the Theseion after the iconography of its reliefs) was constructed. The buildings were aligned along a great drain that can still be traced.

The eastern side of the agora was marked by a monumental colonnade or stoa that was given to the city by Attalos, one of the Hellenistic kings of Pergamom. This has been reconstructed and contains a museum containing the finds from the excavation.

KERAMEIKOS CEMETERY

One of the havens in the busy city is the ancient cemetery lying just outside the Dipylon Gate. The ancient roads spreading out from the gateway were lined with a series of tombs and family plots. Some of the sculptures and finds from the burials are displayed in the small site museum. As the Kerameikos is crossed by a small stream, it acts as a nature reserve.

DELPHI

DELPHI, THE SANCTUARY OF APOLLO, IS LOCATED ON THE SLOPES OF MOUNT PARNASSOS, AND WAS THE HOME OF THE FAMOUS ORACLE.

● **WHERE IS IT?**
In central Greece, inland from Itea on the gulf of Corinth

● **WHEN TO VISIT**
The site is open all year, but can be affected by snow in winter

● **GENERAL INFO**
For further information check online at www.culture.gr

Delphi was one of four sanctuaries where Panhellenic games were celebrated. The fifth-century BC Greek historian Herodotus recounts some of the oracles: about Kroisos from western Turkey, the Athenians on the eve of the Persian invasion and the establishment of Greek colonies.

TEMPLE OF APOLLO

A series of temples have stood on this site; one of the earliest was destroyed by a great fire, which consumed the sanctuary in the mid-sixth century BC. This allowed a refurbishment and expansion of the sanctuary, including the construction of a massive terrace wall that cuts it in half. The Athenians used the wall as the backing for a long colonnade in which they seem to have displayed trophies from the defeat of the Persians.

Herodotus tells us that a new temple was completed at the end of the sixth century. The Alkmaionid family, in exile from Athens, offered to give marble pediments for the temple on the condition that the Delphic oracle asked any visiting Spartans to liberate Athens (and to let the family return).

TREASURY OF THE ATHENIANS

A sacred way zig-zags up the sanctuary starting from an entrance at the southeast corner. The Treasury of the Athenians was constructed at one of the key turns at the western end of the sanctuary. It was decorated with relief panels (metopes) showing the Athenian hero Theseus, as well as the Dorian

Herakles. The Roman travel writer Pausanias suggested that it was constructed after the Battle of Marathon in 490BC.

TREASURY OF THE SIPHNIANS

One of the treasuries mentioned by Herodotus belonged to the Greek island of Siphnos and was reported to have been one of the richest in the

Left: The excavated remains and foundations of the ancient city, situated in the Parnassos Mountains

Below: Bronze charioteer erected to mark a victory in the Pythian Games by one of the tyrants of Sicily in the 470s BC

sanctuary. This is traditionally associated with a building that stood in the southern part of the sanctuary that carried a continuous Ionic frieze (now housed in the site museum). It showed the battle between the gods and giants, including a chariot drawn by lions. A pair of caryatids (architectural sculptures of women acting as columns) was placed at the front of the treasury.

PLATAIA MONUMENT

Just to the east of the temple is a circular base. This is where the members of the Hellenic league against the Persians dedicated a massive bronze cauldron supported by twisted snakes. The tripod was removed in antiquity to Byzantium (Istanbul) where it was placed inside the Hippodrome, and it remains there today.

Knossos

WHERE IS IT?
About 5km (3 miles) south of Heraklion, Crete (Greece), on the road to Archanes

WHEN TO VISIT
The palace is open all year round, except public holidays, although there are restricted opening hours in the winter

GENERAL INFO
The finds from Knossos are exhibited at the Archaeological Museum of Heraklion

KNOSSOS

THE BRONZE AGE SITE AT KNOSSOS IS THE LARGEST AND MOST SIGNIFICANT OF THE MINOAN PALACES. AS HOME OF THE LEGENDARY KING MINOS, KNOSSOS IS ASSOCIATED WITH SEVERAL GREEK MYTHS, MOST NOTABLY THE FEARSOME TALE OF THE LABYRINTH, HOME OF THE MINOTAUR.

Right: The Palace of Minos, the multi-storied Bronze Age residence of King Minos

The substantial reconstructions of the palace by Sir Arthur Evans following his excavations in the early part of the 20th century, provide an impression of the extent and opulence of the Minoan buildings. However, the Minoan era (from about 3000BC) is only part of the story, and Knossos enjoyed a long and frequently prosperous history both before and after the Minoan era.

DISCOVERY AND EXCAVATION

The first Minoan remains at Knossos were brought to light in 1878 by the appropriately-named Minos

Kalokaironos. Although several other archaeologists attempted to commence subsequent investigations at Knossos, it was Sir Arthur Evans, curator of the Ashmolean Museum in Oxford, who acquired the estate that included the Knossos site. Work began at Knossos at 11am on 23 March 1900, and the first artefacts were exhibited in London in 1903.

Above: The palace throne room, Knossos

THE PEOPLE OF KNOSSOS

The first settlers arrived at Knossos in about 7000BC, and established their homes on the site of what was to become the later Minoan palace. This area continued to be inhabited until about 1360BC, when the palace was destroyed by fire and never rebuilt. Although the surrounding area flourished for another 2,000 years, the palace site was never re-inhabited, possibly because of its supposed associations with the Minotaur myth. The Romans established a colony slightly to the north of the palace site, which became one of the main Roman cities on Crete. It is not surprising that the emperor Hadrian, a renowned admirer of all things Greek, favoured Knossos, no doubt in part due to its past associations.

PALACE OF MINOS

The main focus of interest for today's visitor is the Bronze Age palace. The use of the term 'palace' is somewhat misleading; in addition to being a residence, archaeology suggests that the palace was the economic, religious, creative and administrative focus of a series of states, not unlike the Greek cities of the classical period. In addition to having extensive archives, written in the still undeciphered Linear A script, the palace supported a large number of specialist artisans, best known for their production of a remarkable series of wall paintings, now sadly fragmentary remains, which decorated various areas of the palace. There were also extensive storage facilities for goods of all kinds. This era came to a violent and abrupt end around 1500BC, when many of the major sites on Crete, including the palace at Knossos, were destroyed by fire. Shortly afterwards, the palace was rebuilt and reoccupied, seemingly by Mycenaean invaders, and many of the remains that can be seen at Knossos date from this period.

THESEUS AND THE MINOTAUR

The palace at Knossos is associated with several fascinating Greek myths and legends, including the story of the slaughter of the Minotaur at the hands of Theseus, prince of Athens. King Minos, who was enraged by the murder of his son by the King of Athens, ordered his fleet to sail to Athens and take the city. Rather than destroy Athens, Minos chose to exact a cruel revenge—a tribute of 14 young Athenians, to be imprisoned in a labyrinth, a maze-like creation of the architect Daidalos. Their fate was to be fed to the Minotaur, a creature that was part man, part bull, the offspring of an unnatural union between Minos' wife, Pasiphaë, and a beautiful white bull from the sea. Wishing to kill the Minotaur, Theseus willingly offered to be part of the tribute. Theseus killed the Minotaur and escaped the Labyrinth thanks to Ariadne, daughter of Minos.

Left: Hanging on the walls inside the Palace of Minos is a remarkable series of wall paintings

Below: Wall paintings depicting the bull leapers of Knossos

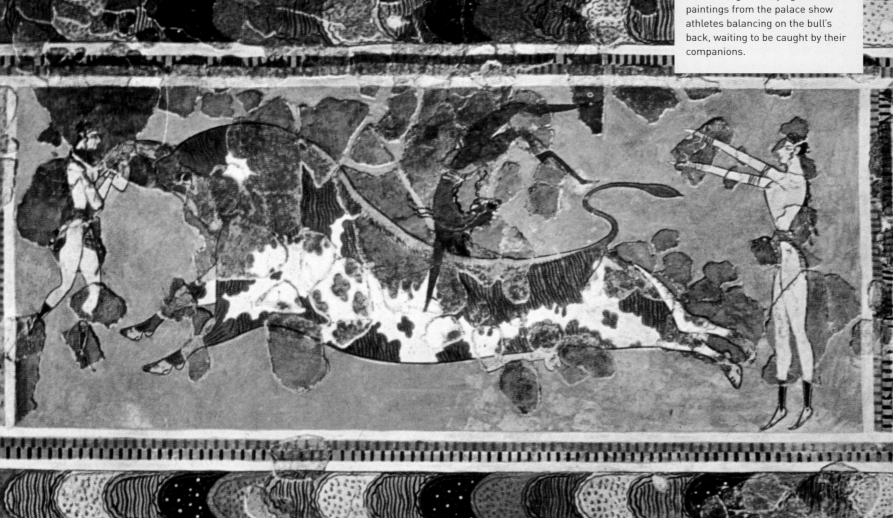

Mycenae

WHERE IS IT?

About 2km (1 mile) from the modern village bearing the same name, which is itself about 2km (1 mile) from the main road between Corinth and Argos (Greece)

WHEN TO VISIT

The site and museum are open all year round, except public holidays, although restricted opening hours apply in winter

GENERAL INFO

The museum is small and usually very busy. Try to time your visit either early in the morning or late in the afternoon. Local buses from Nafplion stop at the village, although buses from Athens usually stop on the main road, at the turning for the village

MYCENAE

THE FORTIFIED CITADEL OF MYCENAE WAS THE MAIN CENTRE OF THE BRONZE AGE CIVILIZATION OF MAINLAND GREECE. MYCENAE HAS ALSO BEEN IMMORTALIZED IN LEGEND—IN HOMER'S EPIC POEM THE ILIAD, MYCENAE WAS THE HOME OF KING AGAMEMNON, GENERAL OF THE ACHAEAN ARMIES AGAINST THE TROJANS.

Although there had been occupation on the citadel of Mycenae from the seventh millennium BC onwards, the visible remains on site date from the 16th to 13th centuries BC. In addition to two Grave Circles, funerary enclosures containing lavish burials, there is the heraldic Lion Gate, together with the massive fortifications and remains of the palace, associated in legend with the murder of Agamemnon by his wife Clytemnestra, as dramatized in the *Oresteia* by Aeschylus.

'WELL-BUILT MYCENAE'

Visitors to the site are immediately reminded of the Homeric epithet, 'Well-Built Mycenae'. The citadel is surrounded by impressive walls built in the technique known as Cyclopean, as it was believed by the ancient Greeks that the stones were so large they must have been moved by the Cyclopes, a race of one-eyed giants.

Other impressive evidence of engineering skills is the secret cistern, which ensured the inhabitants of Mycenae would not be without water in the event of siege. Bring a torch if you wish to take the steep, and sometimes rather slippery, steps down to the cistern.

THE TREASURY OF ATREUS

Outside the citadel itself is the tomb known as the Treasury of Atreus, built in about 1250BC. Already plundered when visited by the Roman traveller Pausanias in the second century AD, it was once believed that such tombs were storehouses for valuables. Consisting of a round chamber (the tholos, from which this type of tomb is named) approached by an unroofed passage lined with dressed stone, the tomb is a remarkable feat of engineering. The chamber is constructed of 33 courses of dressed stone, fitted so that each course slightly overlaps the one below it, with the uppermost course being closed with a single block. The overlapping sections have been removed, so that the interior appears smooth and unbroken. The elaborate decoration of the tomb's exterior, now scattered in several museums, suggests that the original appearance of the building must have been spectacular. No doubt the looted grave offerings would have been equally stunning.

Left: Grave Circle A

MYCENAE 'RICH IN GOLD'

The Homeric epithet 'rich in gold' was confirmed by Heinrich Schliemann's discovery in 1876 of graves with offerings suggesting they were the final resting place of the early rulers of Mycenae. The offerings included bronze weapons and quantities of jewellery, some probably worn in life. Other gold items were made for the funeral, such as the five spectacular masks and discs from burial shrouds. The initial sight of the body seemingly clothed in gold, wearing a gold headdress and jewellery, must have been truly magnificent.

Right: Funerary mask, formerly thought to be that of Agamemnon, in the National Archaeological Museum, Athens

OLYMPIA

THE SANCTUARY OF ZEUS WAS THE HOME OF THE OLYMPIC
GAMES, TRADITIONALLY ESTABLISHED IN 776BC. THE
PINE-CLAD HILLS AND THE STADIUM EVOKE THE BIRTH OF
SPORTING HISTORY.

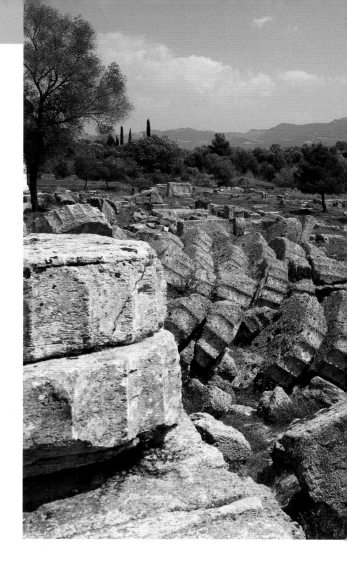

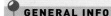
Olympia

WHERE IS IT?

In the western Peloponnese,
Greece

GENERAL INFO

For further information and
opening times of the site and
museum see www.culture.gr

**Right: Fallen pillars from the
Temple of Zeus**

The sanctuary of Zeus was positioned at the confluence
of the rivers Alpheios and Kladeos. Just to the north of
the sanctuary is the small hill known as the Kronion.
Outside the sanctuary proper was a gymnasium and
other administrative buildings.

TEMPLE OF ZEUS

The Temple of Zeus was constructed during the
fifth century BC. It was made of local stone, but
was decorated with imported marble statues in
the pediments and the metopes. The main eastern
pediment showed the myth associated with the
foundation of the games: the chariot race between
Pelops (whose name is found in the Peloponnese) and
Oinomaos. The western pediment showed the rape
of the Lapith women; the Athenian hero Theseus is
shown wielding an axe near the centre. The metopes
at each end of the temple show the deeds conducted
by Herakles.

WORKSHOP OF PHEIDIAS

The colossal gold and ivory cult statue of Zeus was
a later addition to the temple, made by the Athenian
sculptor Pheidias, probably after finishing the Athena
Parthenos at Athens. The statue was described by the
Roman travel writer Pausanias, and it showed the god
seated on his throne. (One ancient writer suggested
that if he stood up, Zeus would push his way through
the roof!).

The statue was made in a special workshop just
to the west of the sanctuary, but with the same
proportions as the inner part of the Temple of Zeus.
(The workshop was later converted into a Byzantine
church.) German excavators found moulds and
fragments from the statue. One of the finds was a
plain black-glossed mug inscribed with the name
of Pheidias.

STADIUM

The stadium lay to the east of the sanctuary and was
joined to it by a short tunnel. Remains of the start and
finishing lines have been found. These give a distance

PHILIP OF MACEDON

Once Philip II had defeated the Greeks at the Battle of Chaironeia in 338BC, he constructed a round temple (a tholos) in the northwest corner of the sanctuary. This contained gold and ivory statues of the Macedonian royal family, including Alexander the Great.

Below: Detail of the bearded head of a sculpture of Zeus in the site museum

of 192.8m (630ft), the length of an ancient *stade* (which provides the name stadium). The sloping banks surrounding the running track could have seated some 45,000 people. The judges had a special enclosure in the middle of the south side of the track

TREASURIES

Olympia drew contestants from across the Greek world. Individual cities constructed a series of treasuries on a low terrace at the northeast corner of the sanctuary. Among them are cities from Greek colonies in the west: Syracuse, Selinunte and Metapontum. The buildings were probably for storing dedications.

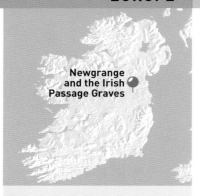

WHERE IS IT?

64 km (40 miles) north of Dublin, Republic of Ireland, and easily visited on a day trip driving north on the M1 or N2 highways, following the signs to the visitor centre.

WHEN TO VISIT

Visitor centre open daily 9.30–5.30 (9–7 in high season)
Newgrange open all year; Knowth open Easter–end Oct

GENERAL INFO

Shuttle buses take visitors to Newgrange and Knowth, where there is no private vehicular access. Average time for visit: exhibition one hour; exhibition and Newgrange two hours, exhibition, Newgrange and Knowth three hours

NEWGRANGE AND THE IRISH PASSAGE GRAVES

NEWGRANGE IS A TYPE OF BURIAL MONUMENT KNOWN AS A PASSAGE GRAVE, IN WHICH LARGE FLAT STONES WERE USED TO CONSTRUCT A BURIAL CHAMBER AND A TUNNEL LEADING INTO IT, ALL OF WHICH WAS COVERED BY A MOUND OF SMALL STONES AND EARTH.

Right: The reconstructed façade at the Newgrange passage grave

Passage graves are one of several types of megalithic tombs found in Ireland and in other parts of western Europe. The megalithic tombs of Ireland were built by Neolithic people over a period of around 1,000 years beginning sometime before 3500BC, with the most impressive being constructed between about 3300 and 2900BC. These farmers and stockherders had elaborate rituals surrounding the transition from life into death, which archaeologists are only just beginning to unravel. Each element of the tombs, from the architecture to the placement of the bones and ashes of the dead, had tremendous meaning for the prehistoric communities that built these monuments. Often the stones are decorated with complex designs whose location within the tomb was deliberately chosen.

IRISH GRAVES AND MONUMENTS

The Irish passage graves primarily occur in a band across the island from the northwest corner near Sligo to the east coast around Dublin, with some outliers to the north and south. They are often found in clusters, and four such passage grave cemeteries stand out from the rest: Loughcrew with over 30 tombs; the Bend of the Boyne complex with 35–40 tombs in County Meath; Carrowkeel with 14 tombs; and Carrowmore with originally up to 100 tombs (many have been destroyed) in County Sligo. Elsewhere smaller

cemeteries and individual monuments, such as the Mound of the Hostages on the Hill of Tara, dot the landscape. The builders of passage graves often liked to situate them on hills or ridgelines. In areas where passage graves appear on the map to be dispersed, such as in County Wicklow, they actually form networks of tombs on mountain tops which are all visible from each other.

NEWGRANGE

Newgrange is probably the most famous Irish passage grave and the one most visited by tourists due to its proximity to Dublin. After excavations in the 1970s, the tomb was reconstructed in a style that may have some archaeological justification but whose execution seems fanciful, even garish. It is indeed an immense passage grave, with a circular mound 85m (279ft) in diameter and 11m (36ft) high. From an entrance in the façade, its passage leads 19m (62ft) into the main burial chamber. From the central chamber, 5.2m (17ft) by 6.6m (21.6ft), smaller chambers branch off, while its domed roof is built up of flat stones in circular courses, each one set closer to the centre until they reach a peak 6m (19.6ft) above the floor.

SUN'S ALIGNMENT

The most remarkable aspect of Newgrange is the fact that, on the winter solstice, the rays of the rising sun shine though an opening above the passage entrance and illuminate the passage all the way into the central chamber. For just 17 minutes at sunrise on 21 December, direct sunlight can enter the tomb only through the opening over the door. Clearly this moment held meaning for the Neolithic builders of Newgrange, and they deliberately oriented the passage towards the southeast and constructed the special opening in order to catch the morning light.

KNOWTH

Not far from Newgrange lies Knowth, which has also been excavated and reconstructed but in a more subtle style. The main mound at Knowth is 80m (262ft) by 95m (312ft) with 127 kerbstones around its periphery. Many of the kerbstones are decorated with elaborate carved designs. The mound contains two passage graves, back to back, one entering from the east side and one from the west. In the eastern grave, a 35m (115ft) passage leads to a cruciform chamber, while in the western grave a 32m (105ft) passage ends in a rectangular chamber. Around the main mound at Knowth are 19 smaller satellite tombs with passages and chambers. One of the most spectacular artefacts from Knowth, which was found in the eastern grave, is a stone macehead, thought to have come from Scotland, decorated with curvilinear carvings. The macehead is on display in the National Museum in Kildare Street, Dublin.

Left: Inside the magnificent Newgrange passage grave

Below: Detail of the inscribed stones that can be found at the back of the Newgrange burial mound

Skellig
Michael

WHERE IS IT?

12km (7 miles) off the coast of
County Kerry, Republic of Ireland

WHEN TO VISIT

Subject to good weather, boat trips
run daily from April to September

GENERAL INFO

Tourist access has been restricted
for conservation purposes but
guided tours can be booked

SKELLIG MICHAEL

THE IRISH MONASTERY OF SKELLIG MICHAEL, 'MICHAEL'S ROCK' IN ENGLISH, WAS FOUNDED IN AD588 BY CHRISTIAN MONKS. A HANDFUL OF MONKS LIVED HERE FOR SIX CENTURIES BEFORE REJOINING A MONASTERY ON THE MAINLAND AT BALLINSKELLIGS IN THE 12TH CENTURY. APART FROM THE KEEPERS OF THE TWO 19TH-CENTURY LIGHTHOUSES, IT HAS BEEN UNINHABITED SINCE.

Early Christian monks followed the example of the 3rd-century AD St. Anthony and other Ethiopian and Egyptian saints who withdrew into the desert. Religious asceticism underpins the choice of the remote island of Skellig Michael and the placing of buildings. Most striking are the remains of a hermitage constructed 220m (722ft) above the sea on the island's South Peak. This was accessible only by a tortuous route that cut through a rock chimney known as 'The Needle's Eye' and along sections of perilously narrow path. It is likely that one of the hermitage terraces could have been a garden.

INACESSIBILITY OF SKELLIG MICHAEL'S RELIGIOUS BUILDINGS

The monastery was built on a rocky shelf, sloping at 45 degrees, on the eastern side of the Northeast peak. A medieval church probably dates to the late 10th or early 11th century. Other ruined structures on the island include two oratories and six beehive-shaped monastic huts, or *clochans,* that perched above sheer cliffs. Two stone water cisterns stored rainwater. Several *leachts*, structures similar to cairns, have been identified. *Leachts* are common but enigmatic features of medieval religious sites, perhaps marking burial places or serving as altars.

Local stone was used to build the *leachts* and drystone walling. The terrain required skilfully built retaining walls to support the buildings and terracing. Three terraces were built at different stages of the ascent and to level the ground for building on. The fill for the South Peak hermitage terrace would have had to be hauled up by rope through the Needle's Eye. A stone slab carved with a cross within a circle (a Celtic cross) was discovered on the oratory terrace in 1982, and although its function is unknown, it is thought similar stones may have been used to mark graves.

Left: Beehive huts, a distinctive landmark of the monastic origins at Skellig Michael

Above: Skellig Michael, a lonely place perched high above the cliffs

DEFENSIVE MEASURES

Despite the island's rugged terrain, it was vulnerable to invasion. The monastery could be reached from sea level by three stone stairways. Only the hermitage was easily defensible and the monastic population was probably never more than about a dozen. Contemporary texts mention repeated Viking raids during the early to mid-9th century, probably in the mistaken belief that monasteries contained valuable and precious objects. One tells of an abbot named Etgal who was carried off and starved in captivity.

Alpine Rock Art

ALPINE ROCK ART

THOUGH FAMOUS FOR ITS PALAEOLITHIC ART SITES, EUROPE HAS A WEALTH OF LATER ROCK ART IN THE FORM OF INCISED AND CARVED IMAGES AND FORMS, FOUND THROUGHOUT THE ALPS.

WHERE IS IT?
The Naquane Rock Art Park is near Capo di Ponte, northeast of Brescia, in Lombardy, northern Italy

WHEN TO VISIT
Petroglyphs can be viewed daily except Monday

GENERAL INFO
Adjoining are other parks including the Regional Reserve of Rock Art Engravings of Ceto-Cimbergo-Paspardo (entrance at Nadro di Ceto) and Foppe di Nadro

HOW OLD?
Petroglyphs are notoriously difficult to date, and age estimates are based largely on subject matter and style. Where images have been engraved over other figures, sequences and relative, ages can be deduced.

The highest concentrations of sites occur at Valcamonica (Camonica Valley) in Italy and on Monte Bego in the French Maritime Alps (southeastern France). At Valcamonica, there are hundreds of thousands of incised and pecked (hammered) images along a 40km (25 mile) stretch. The figures were made on sandstone boulders, over a time span of perhaps 8,000 years.

PETROGLYPHS

A few petroglyphs from these sites may date to the end of the Palaeolithic, as well as the Neolithic (about 4000–3000BC), whereas some date to Roman and medieval times. Images of men with weapons such as daggers and axes suggest that the makers had metallurgical knowledge. Some of these objects are very similar to artefacts excavated from Copper, Bronze and Iron Age sites. About 80 per cent of the imagery probably dates to the Iron Age (c2800 years ago until the Romans conquered the local people, the Camunni, in AD16). The petroglyphs include isolated single figures as well as elaborate compositions and complex accumulations of imagery comprising several hundred figures.

NAQUANE

About 104 engraved rocks can be seen at the Naquane Rock Art Park (Valcamonica). The animals represented are those local to the area, including chamois and deer, with dogs and horses appearing in the Iron Age petroglyphs. Amongst the man-made objects depicted

are forms interpreted as steep-roofed granaries, ploughs and carts. Some apparently abstract designs may be topographical figures (maps). Others, such as circles with radiating lines reminiscent of the sun and enigmatic figures known as Camunnian roses, are interpreted as symbols of unknown religious significance.

Human figures occur throughout the sequence. The Neolithic human images include simple figures with bent knees and raised arms, interpreted by some as 'praying figures' (oranti). The later art includes armed warriors, duels and hunting scenes that may have had ritual significance, perhaps in young men's initiation ceremonies. Footprints are also present.

MONTE BEGO

At Monte Bego on the French-Italian border, about 35,000 images have been recorded in the Mercantour National Park, in two valleys, Meraviglie (Les Merveilles) and Fontanalba. The imagery is comparable in many ways with that of Valcamonica, though the range of imagery is more restricted, being mostly weapons and ox-drawn ploughs. It is thought most were made during the Copper Age (following the Neolithic) and the Bronze Age, a period of about 800 years. It has been suggested that the density of imagery may relate to a special regard for the mountain as a sacred place.

Right: Petroglyphs of deer at Valcamonica

Cerveteri &
Tarquinia

CERVETERI AND TARQUINIA

THE ETRUSCAN CITIES OF CAERE (THE ROMAN NAME FOR CERVETERI) AND TARQUINIA ARE FAMOUS FOR THEIR CEMETERIES AND DECORATED TOMBS.

WHERE IS IT?
In Tuscany, north of Rome (Italy)

WHEN TO VISIT
The sites are open all year but hours are restricted

GENERAL INFO
Finds are housed in local museums and the Villa Giulia, Rome

The extensive cemeteries of the Etruscan cities to the north of Rome provide impressive iconography dating back to the seventh and sixth centuries BC, and reflect an important culture that flourished before Rome started to dominate the Italian peninsula.

CERVETERI

Cerveteri, known to the Greeks as Agylla, and the Romans as Caere, was a major city covering some 150ha (370 acres). There were two main cemeteries, now known by the modern names of Bandiataccia and Monte Abatone. The Regolini-Galassi tomb, dating to the middle of the seventh century BC, contained silver bowls (perhaps reflecting influences from the eastern Mediterranean) and fine gold-work pointing towards the wealth of the Etruscan elites in this period. Such elite burials can clearly be seen in the Bandiataccia cemetery where the earliest tombs, dating to the seventh century BC, were placed under monumental circular burial mounds. However by the end of the sixth century BC, and certainly by the middle of the fifth, rows of uniform stone-fronted tombs were constructed. During this period elite graves seem to have been constructed in new areas. The Tomb of the Reliefs, dating from the mid-fourth century BC, is carved like a dining room with couches that have stone cushions for the dead; armour and drinking vessels were hung on the walls.

TARQUINIA

Ancient writers such as Pliny the Elder (dAD79) described panel paintings (now lost). However it is possible to get a hint of the expertise in ancient painting from the decorated tombs discovered at Tarquinia. The tombs were cut into the tufa and the

Left: Detail of carving on columns belonging to the Tomb of the Reliefs, Cerveteri

Right: Etruscan musicians, a copy of a 5th-century BC fresco in the Tomb of the Leopard at Tarquinia

paint applied to a plaster finish. Some of the themes pick up on the mourning. For example in the Tomb of the Auguri, dating to the end of the sixth century, two mourners, each with a hand raised in grief, stand either side of a closed (and painted) doorway. The same tomb also showed two naked wrestlers, presumably taking part in some funerary games; their prize of metal bowls is shown stacked between them. The Tomb of the Triclinium shows individuals dancing to the sound of music played on a double flute.

PYRGI

The harbour settlement of Cerveteri was located at Pyrgi. Some gold plaques, probably dating to around 500BC, were discovered in the temple during excavations in 1964; they carried texts in Etruscan and Phoenician. This showed that the temple was dedicated by Thefarie Velianas, from Cerveteri, to Uni (the Etruscan equivalent of the Roman Juno, the consort of Jupiter) and the Phoenician goddess Astarte. These texts assisted with the reading of Etruscan.

Next spread: Etruscan necropolis, Cerveteri

Greek Temples
of Italy

📍 **WHERE IS IT?**

Temples can be found at Paestum
near Salerno, and on the island of
Sicily at Siracusa, Agrigento and
Selinunte

📍 **WHEN TO VISIT**

Open all year but hours are
restricted

📍 **GENERAL INFO**

For information on Paestum
www.culturacampania.rai.it;
for Agrigento
www.valleyofthetemples.com

GREEK TEMPLES OF ITALY

THE CITIES OF MAINLAND GREECE COLONIZED SOUTHERN ITALY AND SICILY FROM THE EIGHTH CENTURY BC. SOME OF THE MOST STRIKING EXAMPLES OF GREEK TEMPLES CAN BE FOUND IN THE WEST.

One of the most distinctive characteristics of
Greek cities was the worship of the Olympian gods,
and hence the largest temples were normally
associated with the patron deities of the city. Other
cults included Apollo, whose oracle at Delphi often
advised prospective colonists before they left mainland
Greece and the islands for new lands in the west.
Many of the temples were constructed in the Doric
architectural order.

PAESTUM

There are three major Doric temples in the Greek
colony of Poseidonia that was founded around 600BC.
One of the oldest structures, perhaps dating from the
middle of the sixth century, was the Temple of Hera
(the consort of Zeus, the chief deity), known as the
Basilica. It is unusual in having nine columns across
the front (instead of the more usual six). Adjacent to
it, and slightly longer at nearly 60m (197ft), is the

**Right: Remains of an ancient Greek
temple, Temple E at Selinunte, Sicily**

**Far right: Temple of Concord in
Agrigento in the Valley of the Temples,
Sicily**

so-called 'Temple of Poseidon' (though it may have been dedicated to another deity). This was constructed in the first half of the fifth century BC. The third temple, dedicated to Athena, was located to the north of the other two and was slightly smaller at just under 33m (108ft) in length. It was probably constructed around 500BC.

SIRACUSA

One of the oldest Greek colonies was established by the Corinthians at Siracusa in southeastern Sicily; the traditional foundation date for this event was 733BC. It owed its location to the presence of a very fine natural harbour. One of the most striking temples was dedicated to Athena and was some 55m (180ft) in length. It may have been built with the booty taken from the defeat of the Carthaginians by Gelon in the early fifth century BC. The temple was converted into a church and now serves as the duomo; the Doric columns of the Temple of Athena can be clearly seen round the exterior of the building.

AGRIGENTO

The colony of Akrgas lies on the south coast of Sicily and was established in the early sixth century BC. A series of Doric temples were constructed for the city. One of the earliest (Temple A) was constructed by one of the main gates for the city. One of the most complete temples (F, sometimes known as the 'Temple of Concord') dates to the middle of the fifth century BC and was around 38m (125ft) in length. One of the largest, but most fragmentary, was originally dedicated to Olympian Zeus and was just over 110m (360ft) in length.

SELINUNTE

The colony of Selinous was situated in southwestern Sicily and was established around 650BC. Some seven colonnaded temples were constructed here, three on the east side of the site, and four in the west. One of the grandest was the Temple of Apollo (G), identified by an inscription that described the dedication of booty in the 470s BC, and constructed in the late sixth century BC.

DORIC TEMPLES

Doric temples are recognized by the cushion-like capitals at the top of the fluted and tapering columns. Above the columns are square panels (metopes) separated by vertically grooved sections (triglyphs).

OSTIA

THIS HARBOUR CITY OF ROME ORIGINALLY LAY AT THE MOUTH OF THE RIVER TIBER. OSTIA WAS THE MAIN ENTRY POINT FOR FOOD AND OTHER MATERIALS NEEDED FOR THE MASSIVE CITY OF ROME.

WHERE IS IT?
Near Rome (Italy), 30km (19 miles) from the city centre

GENERAL INFO
Useful information can be found at www.ostia-antica.org

The vulnerability of ships from storms encouraged the creation of a permanent artificial harbour that would allow the transhipment of cargoes to the river barges that could then be taken up the Tiber.

THE PIAZZA OF THE CORPORATIONS AND NEARBY STORAGE

The square consists of offices on three sides and the theatre on the fourth. This area reflects the cosmopolitan nature of the city: one of the offices belonged to merchants from Sabratha in modern Libya, which traded in wild animals and ivory.

Ostia was equipped with numerous storehouses to cope with the goods being transferred to Rome. The great Horrea, located next to the Piazza of the Corporations, allowed access from quays on the river. it

Below: Remains of a Corinthian capital

THE MAKING OF CLOTH
Evidence for commercial activity has been uncovered. There were at least seven fulleries in the city, some clearly operating with large numbers of workers. These contained a series of basins in which the textiles were manipulated.

has been estimated that this building alone could have stored nearly seven tonnes of grain. Barracks for some 300 men (guards to respond to the threat of fire) were provided in the city towards the end of the first century AD.

THE TEMPLES

The main public space in Ostia was the forum. On the north side was a large temple on a raised podium that dates to the second century AD. It was probably dedicated to Jupiter and his consort Juno as well as Minerva. On the south side of the forum was the Temple of Roma (the personification of Rome) and Augustus.

One of the mystery cults to spread from the east related to Mithras. The cult became popular in the second and third centuries AD, and often the temples are associated with military garrisons on Rome's frontiers. However some 15 Mithraea have been identified in Ostia alone. One of the features of the cult was the imagery of Mithras slaying the bull.

THE BATHS AND HOUSING

There are a number of bathhouses in the city. The forum baths were constructed about AD160 and covered over 3,000sq m (32,292sq ft). Inscriptions on the building, as well as the lead piping, show that the benefactor was M. Gavius Maximus. Ostia provides good evidence for private housing, some with multiple storeys. Some were extensive, such as the House of the Columns, constructed during the third century AD, but some of the families lived in smaller apartments.

THE HARBOUR FACILITIES

The harbours are situated on the far, north side of the Tiber from the ancient town. The earliest was constructed by the emperor Claudius and was protected by artificial moles.

The massive Trajanic octagonal harbour, over 700m (2,296ft) across, was constructed in the early years of the second century AD and could contain some 100 ships that unloaded into the warehouses situated behind the quays.

Below: Mosaic work, Piazza of the Corporations

POMPEII/ HERCULANEUM

THESE TWO SMALL TOWNS WERE DESTROYED IN THE GREAT ERUPTION OF VESUVIUS IN AD79, WHICH PROVIDES MANY INSIGHTS INTO ROMAN LIFE.

Pompeii & Herculaneum

WHERE IS IT?
In Campania, 24km (15 miles) from Naples (Italy)

WHEN TO VISIT
The site is open all year; for times see www.culturacampania.rai.it

GENERAL INFO
Finds from the site can be seen in the Archaeological Museum in Naples

Pompeii was destroyed by a series of pyroclastic flows that engulfed the town during the great eruption of Vesuvius in AD79. The city was buried, and the site was only rediscovered in the late 17th century. Excavations began in 1748.

THE FORUM AND THE HOUSE OF THE FAUN

The main public area in any Roman city was the forum, and at Pompeii it is dominated by the Temple of Jupiter. A temple of Apollo was located along the western side. Legal cases were heard in the Basilica, which was placed at the southwestern corner of the forum.

The House of the Faun is one of the largest private residences in Pompeii. Inside was one of the finest mosaics in antiquity, showing Alexander's defeat of the Persian king Darius. The focus of the scenes is Darius in his chariot who points towards Alexander charging across from the left. (The mosaic itself is on display in Naples.) The scale of the house is evocative of a Hellenistic royal palace.

PUBLIC ENTERTAINMENT AND FACILITIES

Evidence for gladiatorial games at Pompeii is provided by the oval amphitheatre, which could seat up to 15,000 spectators. The gladiators were accommodated in barracks near the Stabiae Gate and pieces of gladiatorial armour were found inside. Pompeii had two theatres: the large one seating some 4,000 people, and the adjacent Odeion for around 1,000. A number of thermal baths have been uncovered. These consisted of a series of cold, warm and hot rooms.

GARDENS

One of the features of the excavations has been the means to reconstruct the appearance of ancient gardens. It has been possible to make casts of the roots to work out the type of plants. This has allowed houses to be brought to life showing how the natural world was contained within the formal house.

Left: Well-preserved mosaics in the House of Neptune Amphitrite

Below: A perfectly preserved floor mosaic uncovered at Herculaneum

VILLA OF THE MYSTERIES

The Villa of Mysteries is located outside the city walls. Inside was a continuous frieze of wall paintings, which gives the complex its name. The wall paintings appear to show the initiation into a female mystery cult linked to Dionysos who is shown in the centre—one of the women being initiated is being whipped. It is not clear who would have used this room or if it reflects the religious views of its owners. Other evidence for similar mystery cults has been found elsewhere in the city. There was a temple of the Egyptian goddess Isis as well as domestic shrines in private houses.

 HERCULANEUM

One of the other towns destroyed in AD79 waś Herculaneum. Excavations have found the carbonized remains of wooden features in the city such as beds and doors. A series of bodies on the then waterfront seem to have been taking refuge during the eruption and were killed by one of the pyroclastic flows.

TEMPLES OF MALTA

BETWEEN 3600 AND 2500BC, THE INHABITANTS OF MALTA AND GOZO CONSTRUCTED SOME OF THE MOST IMPRESSIVE PREHISTORIC MONUMENTS IN THE WORLD USING THE MEGALITHIC TECHNIQUE OF EMPLOYING LARGE SLABS OF STONE FOR STRUCTURAL ELEMENTS.

Temples of Malta

WHERE IS IT?

On the Maltese archipelago in the central Mediterranean

WHEN TO VISIT

Restored temples are open all year, but make arrangements to visit underground tombs at Hal Saflieni several weeks in advance (maximum 80 visitors per day)

GENERAL INFO

Admission fees are charged at all sites (one ticket for both Mnajdra and Hagar Qim); see www.heritagemalta.org for opening times and to book visits to Hal Saflieni. Key artefacts and sculptures from the temples and catacombs are on display at the National Museum of Archaeology in Valletta

The island of Malta and the smaller neighbouring island of Gozo saw the construction of some of the earliest freestanding monumental buildings in the world during the late 4th millennium BC. The earliest farmers had cleared the islands of their forests, so for the construction of large monumental structures the inhabitants turned to the limestone bedrock. Slabs were quarried and built into complex structures of interconnected courtyards with semicircular alcoves, or lobes, between 5 and 8m (16 and 26ft) in diameter. These lobed courtyards appear to have been the site for ritual activities, and thus the complexes are called temples despite the fact that we do not know how these rituals were conducted.

TARXIEN

Tarxien is the largest of the Malta temple complexes, and one of the last to be built, around 3000BC. It is located near Valletta, capital of Malta, and was discovered in 1915 by a farmer removing limestone boulders from his field. Tarxien is divided into four major parts, with the South Temple and the Middle Temple being the most significant. Entered through a passage in a limestone façade, the South Temple has elliptical chambers decorated with carved spirals and animals. The lower fragment of an immense statue of a corpulent woman, once 2m (6.5ft) tall, stands to one side. A stone altar held a hidden slot that contained a flint knife, suggesting that sacrifices were performed on it. From one of the lobes of the South Temple, a passage leads to the Middle Temple, the largest unit in the Tarxien complex, 24m (79ft) long with six lobes.

HAL SAFLIENI HYPOGEUM

About 100m (328ft) from the Tarxien temple is the entrance to the Hal Saflieni Hypogeum, catacombs that were hewn from the soft limestone to form an

immense crypt containing the remains of thousands of people. Bodies were buried in niches in over 70 different chambers, while larger spaces appear to have been used for mortuary rituals. Carved decorations on the walls match those seen in the sunlight above at Tarxien.

HAGAR QIM

The best preserved of the Malta temples is found on the south coast at Hagar Qim. Hagar Qim was constructed earlier than the Tarxien complex and is simpler, consisting of one four-lobed temple in a cloverleaf pattern. The interior of Hagar Qim is more constricted than at Tarxien, suggesting that access to it was limited to individuals with special ritual privileges. Large orthostats, or upright stones, define the corners of the Hagar Qim structures. Nearby, the larger Mnajdra complex was built in stages over several centuries resulting in three conjoined units with several lobes.

GGANTIJA, GOZO

Perhaps the oldest of the Maltese temples is found on the smaller island of Gozo, where the double temple at Ggantija, with a façade reaching 8m (26ft) high, adjoins a mortuary complex known as 'the Brochtorff Circle' constructed in natural caves. Construction at Ggantija may have begun as early as 3600BC. The first temple to be built is the larger of the two. Each consists of five lobes connected to a central corridor. Within some of the lobes are niches that resemble closets, formed from upright slabs set into the walls. At Ggantija, the walls of the lobes are built from rough coralline limestone, while the corridors are lined with smooth, pale-yellow Globigerina limestone. Both types are found in the bedrock of Malta, and the builders of the temples clearly made a distinction in where to use each type of stone.

Right: Hagar Qim temple on the island of Malta

Left: Sculpture at Tarxien, believed to be the feet of a female deity

VIKING SWEDEN

SCANDINAVIA WAS THE LAND OF THE VIKINGS DURING THE SECOND HALF OF THE 1ST MILLENNIUM AD AND TRACES OF THEIR ACTIVITY ARE STILL VISIBLE ACROSS THE LANDSCAPE.

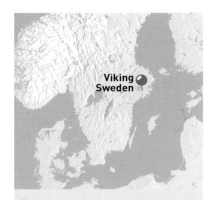

WHERE IS IT?

Birka is 30km (19 miles) west of Stockholm. Ship settings and runestones dot the landscape of Sweden

GENERAL INFO

Almost all archaeological monuments in Sweden are under the protection of the Swedish National Heritage Board (Riksantikvarieämbetet in Swedish, abbreviated RAÄ). The RAA website www.raa.se, with a link to English text, contains information about locations and opening hours of a number of important sites

Right: A setting of standing stones at Kåseberga, known as a 'ship pattern'

Sweden is particularly rich in monuments built by the Vikings and their immediate predecessors, which can be encountered frequently when driving through the countryside. The Swedish Vikings generally looked toward the east and established trade links along the rivers of modern-day Russian and southward to Byzantium.

ANCIENT BIRKA

Birka, on the shores of Lake Mälaren, emerged as an important trading centre late in the 8th century AD and flourished for two centuries before its abandonment. At its peak Birka had about 700 inhabitants who lived in small, closely-packed houses with adjacent workshops. The finds reflect a community that had far-flung trading contacts, all the way to Kiev and Byzantium. Fur was a particularly important commodity: thousands of paw bones from squirrel, fox, and marten testify to the preparation of pelts before being exported.

Around the fortified settlement, thousands of graves contain the remains of its inhabitants. On the nearby island of Adelsö, the local kings and their retainers resided and were buried.

STANDING STONES AND ANCIENT RUNES

Throughout Sweden and neighbouring countries there are upright stones decorated with runes, the alphabet used to write the languages of northern Europe during the late 1st millennium AD. One of the most famous

is the Rök runestone, located just north of the town of Ödeshög, east of Lake Vättern. Drive north on Route 50 and turn off at Alvastra. The Rök stone stands about 1.5m (5ft) tall and is covered with about 280 runic characters on the front and 450 on the back, the longest known runic inscription. It was erected by a man named Varin during the 9th century AD to commemorate his dead son, but the text contains many mythical and epic allusions that have resulted in numerous different scholarly interpretations.

SWEDISH SHIP SETTINGS

Some of the most spectacular structures built during the 1st millennium AD in Sweden are the so-called 'ship patterns'. Patterns of standing stones in which two rows of stones diverge from a point at one end and converge at a point at the other, creating an arrangement that when viewed from above suggests the outline of a ship. Often taller stones are set toward the 'prow' and the 'stern' to emphasize the form of the vessel. Many of the Swedish ship settings apparently were built just before the Viking age, but they would have been prominent features of the landscape in Viking times. The largest one on mainland Sweden is at Kåseberga on the south coast on a headland 10km (6 miles) east of Ystad, overlooking the Baltic Sea. Known as 'Ales stenar' or 'Ale's Stones', this monument is 67m (220ft) long and 19m (62ft) wide at its midsection.

THE ANUNDSHÖG COMPLEX

At Anundshög in central Sweden, a complex of burial mounds, runestones and ship settings was constructed between AD500 and 1100. The largest mound is 10m (33ft) high and 60m (197ft) in diameter. From its top, the visitor can look down on two ship settings, placed stem-to-stern, one 51m (167ft) and the other 54m (177ft) long. Nearby is a row of 14 standing stones that mark the route of an ancient road. The Anundshög complex lies along the main road just east of the city of Västerås.

Although the Viking age ended in the 11th century AD with the arrival of Christianity and political unification, it left its monuments spread across the landscapes of Sweden and neighbouring countries where they remain visible today. Buried Viking finds turn up frequently, especially hoards of silver coins minted as far away as Damascus and Baghdad.

Left: Grave field at Anundshög in Sweden

Right: The rune stone at Rök, Östergötland

Bath

Below: The Roman baths, a UNESCO World Heritage Site

BATH

NESTLING IN THE HEART OF REGENCY BATH ARE THE REMAINS OF A MINERAL-BATH COMPLEX CONSTRUCTED BY THE ROMANS.

The water from the hot mineral spring was collected in a large lead-lined reservoir. This appears to have attracted attention as a place of veneration and 'pilgrims' dropped offerings into the water. One of the finds from the spring was a lead curse tablet relating to the abduction of a woman, Vilbia. The water was then fed into a substantial bathing complex, of which the central feature was a stepped pool. The clearing of the pool uncovered remains of the original Roman roof, containing box tiles to reduce the weight.

TEMPLE OF SULIS MINERVA

The local deity Sulis was combined with the Roman godess Minerva. The temple, first identified by diggings in the area in 1790, was constructed in a classical style on a raised podium. Four Corinthian columns stood at the top of a flight of steps. One of the triangular pediments was decorated with the gorgon mask usually associated with the female deity Minerva—but the moustache on the face reflects the local deity. Thus there would have been a blending of the formal Roman architectural style, with the distinctive local nature of the cult of Sulis.

THE TEMPLE PRECINCT

The space around the temple would have contained the altar where animals would have been sacrificed. Excavations next to the altar recovered the base of a statue with a carefully cut inscription; the dedicator is described as a haruspex, a Roman priest who inspected the insides of sacrificed animals.

INSCRIPTIONS

A number of Latin inscriptions are displayed in the museum attached to the Roman baths. Several of the tombstones suggest that retired legionaries had settled at Bath. Gaius Curiatius Saturninus, a centurion from the II Augustan legion, made a dedication to Sulis Minerva (the cult associated with the worship of the Roman imperial family); his legionary base was at Caerleon, near Newport, on the opposite side of the Severn estuary. A stonemason called Priscus appears to have come from the area round Chartres in northern France, and a Peregrinus, son of Secundus, came from Trier in Germany. All these hint at the cosmopolitan nature of the Roman city.

Right: Gorgon's head

OTHER REMAINS

Many of the Roman remains are covered by the later Regency buildings in Bath. Excavations on Upper Borough Walls were able to reveal a section through the Roman defences that probably can be dated to the second or third centuries AD (traces of the medieval wall can still be seen on the north side of the road). A tessellated pavement remains in situ in one of the basement stairwells of the Mineral Water Hospital, also on Upper Borough Walls; permission needs to be sought to view. It appears to be part of a large urban Roman house.

Caernarfon
Castle

CAERNARFON CASTLE

CAERNARFON CASTLE IS ONE OF A STRING OF CASTLES BUILT BY EDWARD I. (REIGNED AD1272–1307) AND HIS ARCHITECT JAMES OF ST. GEORGE IN EFFORTS TO SUBDUE THE REBELLIOUS WELSH.

WHERE IS IT?

About 15km (9 miles) southwest of Bangor in North Wales

WHEN TO VISIT

Opening times vary seasonally; see website

GENERAL INFO

The castle is managed by the Welsh Heritage body, Cadw (www.cadw.wales.gov.uk)

SECONDARY ROLE

Caernarfon Castle never became the dynastic seat that it was designed to be, and assumed a lesser defensive role along with the other castles in Edward's 'Ring of Iron'. The castle's defences withstood attacks by the Welsh rebel leader Owain Glyndwr at the beginning of the 15th century, but surrendered to Parliamentary forces in the Civil War.

Unlike the other castles of Edward's 'Ring of Iron', Caernarfon was designed not only for defence but also as a seat of government and as an ostentatiously palatial residence for the new Princes of Wales after Wales was incorporated into England. Edward had defeated the Welsh prince Llewellyn ap Gruffydd, who refused to pay homage to the English, in 1277. A second campaign against the Welsh began in 1282. Construction of Caernarfon Castle began in 1283, the same year that work commenced on two of Edward's other great castles, Conwy and Harlech.

DEFENSIVE POWERS

The castles were built along the coast so that they could be provisioned by sea, thus avoiding ambushes on land. Previous fortifications indicate the site's strategic importance: the Roman fort of Segontium nearby, and in the late 11th century a Norman motte and bailey, part of which was incorporated into the new castle. Building materials for Caernarfon Castle were shipped in, with the principal building work completed within two years. A town and market were incorporated into the design, with the existing Welsh settlement destroyed to make way for it. The combination of one ring of castle defences and another of town walls, surrounded by a moat, provided a double line of protection.

Towers and two gatehouses are positioned along the 6m (19.5ft) thick curtain wall and the walls were decorated with patterned bands of coloured stone. Welsh rebels attacked before the castle was completed so the English added further defences, including the heavily fortified King's Gate. Though never completed, it was designed to have no fewer than six portcullises and five doors to protect the inner wards.

FIT FOR A PRINCE

Caernarfon Castle differs from Edward's other castles in many ways, including its angular, rather than rounded towers, and in aspects of its internal plan. Many of its unusual features are linked to its intended purpose as a residence, royal seat and symbol of English power over the conquered Welsh. Edward may have incorporated deliberate architectural allusions to the might of Rome and Constantinople. The living quarters, especially in the Eagle and Queen's Towers, were especially elaborate, with chapels on each storey. The Eagle Tower is topped with three sets of turrets, each emblazoned with a stone eagle, an emblem of royal power. Edward's son, later Edward II, was born at Caernarfon Castle in 1284 and became the first English Prince of Wales.

Below: Medieval Caernarfon Castle, beside the Menai Strait

HADRIAN'S WALL

THE FRONTIER SYSTEM MARKING THE NORTHERN EDGE OF
THE ROMAN EMPIRE THAT CUTS ACROSS NORTHERN BRITAIN,
HADRIAN'S WALL WAS BUILT BETWEEN WALLSEND ON THE
RIVER TYNE AND BOWNESS ON SOLWAY.

Hadrian's
Wall

WHERE IS IT?
Stretching across Northumberland
and Cumbria in northern England

GENERAL INFO
Some of the larger forts have
set opening hours; for further
information see www.english-
heritage.org.uk

Construction started in AD122 and consisted of a fixed
frontier of a wall protected by a ditch to the north. The
original plan was to have a much wider wall but this
was narrowed; in places it is possible to see a narrow
wall built on broad foundations. The western part of
Hadrian's Wall, essentially the part in Cumbria, was
originally built in turf and only later replaced in stone
(perhaps under Emperor Septimius Severus). The
southern boundary of the frontier was marked by a
flat-bottomed ditch known as the 'vallum'. There was
a small garrison located every 1.6km (1 mile) with two
turrets in-between, and the wall was strengthened by
the construction of larger forts.

The wall was probably intended to fix the limit
of the empire and mark the end of expansion. Yet
within a generation the emperor Antoninus Pius had
constructed a new (and temporary) frontier system
between the Firth of Forth and the Firth of Clyde in
Scotland (known as the Antonine Wall).

HOUSESTEADS AND CHESTERS

One of the best-preserved infantry forts is located at
Housesteads. Excavations have revealed evidence of
the barracks, granaries and the headquarters building.
Among the visible facilities of the fortress are the
latrines.

The cavalry fort at Chesters was placed next to
the River North Tyne. There was extra stabling for
horses and two additional gates to the north of the

wall, probably to allow the cavalry to sally forth from different points against an enemy. Excavations have revealed a bathhouse complex just outside the fort.

MILECASTLES

These small garrisons were probably intended to house about 80 men. Some of the best-preserved examples are in the central section at Cawfields Crags and just to the west of Housesteads. Each milecastle had a gate that provided access to the north side of the wall. However in some cases this gave access to the edge of the crag, and some of these entrances were later narrowed or blocked. Small inscriptions indicate that Hadrian's Wall was built by men from each of the legionary garrisons of Britain. Each unit seems to have worked on its own designs of milecastles and turrets that have their own characteristics.

VINDOLANDA

The original Roman frontier ran along the line of the Roman road known as the Stanegate. This was garrisoned by a succession of of forts including Vindolanda. Excavations have uncovered waterlogged strata that have allowed organic materials to be preserved. Some of the most important finds are the garrison archives and the personal correspondence of the commander (and his family). These have provided important information about life on the Roman frontier.

MITHRAS

Among the gods worshipped by Roman soldiers was the god Mithras.

One of the best-known temples of Mithras can be seen just outside the fort at Carrawburgh. The altars were dedicated by a series of garrison commanders.

Reconstructions of the Mithraeum can be seen in the Museum of Antiquities at Newcastle University along with other finds from Hadrian's Wall.

Left: A section of Hadrian's Wall on Cuddy's Crag

Below: Housesteads Fort in Northumberland National Park

SKARA BRAE

SKARA BRAE IS A REMARKABLE CLUSTER OF EIGHT INTERCONNECTED STONE HOUSES BUILT OVER 5,000 YEARS AGO IN ONE OF THE MOST REMOTE PARTS OF THE BRITISH ISLES. THE HOUSES ARE FITTED WITH STONE FURNITURE, HEARTHS, AND DRAINS, PROVIDING AN UNUSUAL GLIMPSE OF DOMESTIC LIFE IN THE STONE AGE.

WHERE IS IT?

Along the Bay of Skaill on the west coast of Mainland, Orkney, 31km (19 miles) northwest of Kirkwall (Scotland)

WHEN TO VISIT

Open year-round; April, May and June are the driest months in Orkney

GENERAL INFO

The restored settlement is open to the public. The visitor centre has interpretative exhibits, finds and a café. For further information see www.historic-scotland.gov.uk, www.aboutbritain.com/SkaraBrae.htm

The Orkney Islands, lying just off the northern tip of Scotland, have had very few trees since they emerged from beneath ice sheets at the end of the Ice Age. Yet ancient people were able to adapt to this harsh landscape by building their houses from the most abundant local raw material, slabs of flagstone. One such settlement was built about 5,000 years ago along the Bay of Skaill on the west coast of the largest Orkney island, known as Mainland.

SKARA BRAE REVEALED

After several centuries of habitation, the site was abandoned and covered by drifting sand and sod. A massive storm in 1850 ripped off some of the sod that kept the sand in place, and slowly the stone houses emerged as wind blew the sand away. In the late 1920s, the famous prehistorian V. Gordon Childe carried out excavations at the site, and since then the site has been explored further by other researchers.

Right: Interior showing stone furniture and a central hearth

Far right: Looking out over the Bay of Skaill

THE BUILDING OF SKARA BRAE

The builders of Skara Brae were not the first people to settle along the Bay of Skaill. Earlier inhabitants lived nearby and discarded their rubbish in a large heap called a midden. When construction of the houses began around 3100BC, the builders scooped large pits out of the midden. They then paved the bottoms of the pits with limestone slabs and lined the walls with more rocks to form walls up to 3m (10ft) high. By leaving most of the midden in place around the houses, they insulated the dwelling areas from the fierce winds. Each house is a rectangular structure between 4.5 and 6m (15 and 20ft) across, with a central hearth, connected by passages roofed with stone slabs. How the houses were roofed is a mystery; lacking long timbers, it is possible the builders used whale ribs covered with hides.

STONE FURNITURE

One of the most fascinating aspects of the houses at Skara Brae is the built-in stone fittings that are interpreted as furniture. Slabs of stone were arranged vertically and horizontally to form dressers, while stone boxes lined with seaweed, straw and pelts served as beds. Stone-lined pits in the floors had their joints packed with clay to make them watertight—believed to have been used for storing shellfish.

RELIANT ON SEA AND LAND

Inhabitants of Skara Brae relied on the sea and the land for their livelihood. Fishing was an important source of food, but they also kept cattle and sheep and probably raised a small amount of grain. They also hunted deer and gathered the eggs of seabirds. Stranded whales provided windfalls of meat and blubber. In addition to making grooved pottery, the inhabitants used materials from animals to produce many of their tools and ornaments. Antler and whale ivory were used to make pins and awls, and beads were made from shell and bone. A distinctive type of artefact found at Skara Brae are carved stone balls with ornamented surfaces, often interpreted as symbols of status and power.

SKARA BRAE HERITAGE

After 2500BC, Skara Brae was abandoned and quickly covered over by sand. Today, it is a prominent feature in a cultural landscape that includes several other such stone settlements (although not so well preserved, for they were not embedded in middens), chambered cairns similar to the passage graves of Ireland (see page 76), and stone circles that echo more famous examples like Stonehenge far to the south (see page 108).

WHERE IS IT?

On Salisbury Plain in Wiltshire (England), just west of Amesbury on the A303, abundantly signposted

WHEN TO VISIT

Stonehenge can be visited throughout the year, but best avoid the summer solstice when the site attracts a large and enthusiastic crowd

GENERAL INFO

Although there is no access to the stone circle during normal opening times, access to the stones can be arranged after-hours; see www.english-heritage. org.uk/stonehenge. Allow at least an hour when visiting the stone circle; turn around and gaze upon the surrounding landscape in which abundant, if less visible, archaeological monuments are located

Opposite: Aerial view showing the tenon joints on top of the uprights

Next spread: The stone circle on a bleak winter's day

STONEHENGE

PERHAPS THE MOST RECOGNIZABLE ARCHAEOLOGICAL SITE IN EUROPE, STONEHENGE CONTINUES TO YIELD NEW INFORMATION ABOUT ITS BUILDERS AND THEIR SOCIETY. ALTHOUGH ITS PURPOSE REMAINS A MATTER OF INTENSE ARCHAEOLOGICAL DEBATE, WE KNOW THAT STONEHENGE WAS CONSTRUCTED IN STAGES OVER SEVERAL CENTURIES.

The image of the stone monument is so familiar, photographed from dramatic angles to make it seem more imposing, that the initial impression from a distance is one of disappointment at its diminished scale against the landscape. Only when one draws near does the size of the stones become truly apparent, and one appreciates the accomplishment of the builders in transporting and erecting them.

BUILT IN STAGES

Archaeologists now know that what visitors see today is the final stage in a sequence of monument construction that began around 3000BC. The first stage involved the digging of a circular ditch about 100m (328ft) in diameter to a depth of about 2m (6.5ft) and piling the soil and chalk into an earthen embankment, also about 2m (6.5ft) high. Within this enclosure is a circle of 56 holes, named Aubrey holes after John Aubrey, who found them in the 17th century. Once it was believed the 'Aubrey holes' had been empty or held wooden posts, but recent research has indicated that they were the footings for upright stones, quite possibly bluestones from the Presceli mountains in Wales 370km (230 miles) away. Latest research has indicated that the immense outer continuous circle of stone and lintels known as sarsen stones, and the interior horseshoe of the largest stones with lintels known as trilithons, were erected in the middle of the 3rd millennium BC.

These stones were brought from locations on Salisbury Plain, perhaps from a range of up to 32km (20 miles); transporting and erecting them was a feat of prehistoric engineering. In the five trilithons, the 9-ton lintels are held in place by tenons on the tops of the uprights that fit into mortised holes on the bottoms of the lintels. During the second half of the 3rd millennium, the bluestones were rearranged several times, finally forming a central arc within the sarsen circle.

FINAL RESTING PLACE

Recent excavations have revealed the extent to which Stonehenge was used as a location for the burial of cremated human remains. Over several centuries, dozens of individuals, mostly adults, were buried in and around the monument. One possibility is that these were members of an elite lineage. The astronomical alignment of Stonehenge, in which the sun on the summer solstice rises directly over an outlying stone known as the 'heel stone' and shines into the interior of the monument, must be viewed as part of a complex pattern of mortuary and ceremonial activity.

Stonehenge did not sit alone in the middle of the Salisbury Plain but was part of a larger complex of sites during the 3rd millennium BC. Recent excavations about 3km (2 miles) away at Durrington Walls have revealed the traces of a settlement, and it is believed hundreds more houses lie buried in the area.

Sutton Hoo

WHERE IS IT?

In southeast Suffolk (England), along the River Deben, 14.5km (9miles) northeast of Ipswich; follow signs from the A12 north of Woodbridge

WHEN TO VISIT

The site and visitor centre are open year-round but sometimes only weekends; see the schedule at www.nationaltrust.org.uk/main/w-vh/w-visits/w-findaplace/w-suttonhoo/

GENERAL INFO

In addition to the burial mounds themselves, the visitor centre has interpretative exhibits and events. See also www.suttonhoo.org/. Major finds are on display in the British Museum in London

SUTTON HOO

THE RICHEST ANGLO-SAXON BURIAL SITE IN ENGLAND WAS DISCOVERED IN THE SUMMER OF 1939 UNDER A MOUND NEAR IPSWICH. DATING TO BETWEEN AD550 AND 650, IT IS BELIEVED TO BE THE GRAVE OF AN ANGLO-SAXON KING WHO WAS BURIED IN A SHIP ALONG WITH GOLD AND SILVER JEWELLERY, WOODEN OBJECTS, METAL BOWLS, COINS AND WEAPONS.

In the late summer of 1939, with war clouds gathering across Europe, the attention of the British archaeological community was focused on a cluster of low mounds along the river Deben in southeast Suffolk. A team of archaeologists, aided by local assistants, had discovered a remarkable burial from the first millennium AD. The discovery was special not just because of the immense number of luxury items buried in the chamber but also due to the fact that the entire tomb was contained within a ship.

BASIL BROWN

When Basil Brown, a local archaeologist, began his excavation that summer, he soon noticed rivets

arranged evenly in rows. He had encountered such rivets in earlier excavations of other mounds on the site, and he knew that they were the type used to hold together the planks of ships during the first millennium AD. Brown carefully noted the position of each rivet and left it in place, and as he proceeded lower and lower, he found more such rows. After a while, Brown stepped back and saw that he had found the outline of a ship 27m (89ft) long. Its planks had long since decayed, but the rivets remained in place to show where they had been. Brown's discovery is considered to be one of the masterworks of archaeological excavation and observation.

TREASURE BURIED IN A SHIP

In the centre of the ship was a trove of objects that had been buried with the cremated individual, and archaeological help arrived from across England as the 1939 summer waned. During the last three weeks of July, a total of 263 artefacts were excavated from the middle of the ship. Iron objects included a helmet, a coat of mail, a hammer-axe, and a sword. Gold shoulder clasps were inset with glass and garnets, while a purse with gold decoration held 37 Frankish gold coins. Silver bowls were stacked ten deep, while a large silver dish 70cm (27.5in) in diameter was stamped with the name of the Byzantine emperor Anastasius who ruled between AD491 and 518. Silver spoons were inscribed in Greek, and drinking horns had silver fittings. Celtic and even North African bronze bowls were found alongside a wooden shield with bronze decoration. A wooden lyre, wooden tubs and buckets and woollen textiles completed the inventory.

Left: A low mound forming part of the Sutton Hoo burial site

Right: The Anglo-Saxon helmet found buried in the Sutton Hoo ship

A ROYAL GRAVE

Who might have commanded the power and prestige that resulted in being buried with such lavish goods? Some historians have proposed that the person buried in the Sutton Hoo ship was Raedwald, king of East Anglia from AD599 to 625. Archaeologists are more cautious of identifying the site with a particular historical figure.

TINTERN ABBEY

THE RUINS OF TINTERN ABBEY AND ITS GOTHIC CHURCH ARE ALL THAT REMAIN OF BRITAIN'S SECOND-OLDEST CISTERCIAN MONASTERY, FOUNDED IN AD1131 BY THE LORD OF CHEPSTOW.

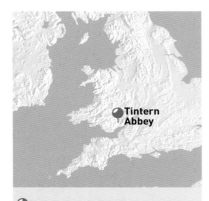

WHERE IS IT?
The Wye Valley in Monmouthshire, on the Welsh–English border. It is 8km (5 miles) north of Chepstow

WHEN TO VISIT
Opening times vary seasonally

GENERAL INFO
Tintern Abbey is managed by the Welsh Heritage body, Cadw (www. cadw.wales.gov.uk)

The Cistercian abbey of Tintern became a casualty of Henry VIII's Dissolution of the Monasteries, surrendering its valuables to the king's treasury in 1536. Lead was stripped from the roofs and sold, and the building fell into ruin.

TINTERN'S WEALTH

The Cistercians, known as 'White Monks' from their undyed wool habits, were an order dedicated to an austere life of poverty, silence, prayer and work. It is estimated that Tintern housed perhaps 20 monks and 50 lay brothers. Tintern prospered thanks to a succession of wealthy patrons. Roger of Bigod, who had enabled rebuilding of the church, endowed the abbey with a Norfolk estate that generated additional income. Like other Cistercian abbeys, Tintern relied heavily on its lay brothers, who worked as agricultural labourers, artisans and shepherds of the monastery's large flocks.

ABBEY BUILDINGS

Only traces remain of the first buildings, the cloisters and domestic buildings being rebuilt in the 13th century, followed by the 72m (236ft) long, red sandstone church. The church was consecrated in 1301, some 30 years after rebuilding began. The floor plan is cruciform, with an aisled nave and chapels in the two transepts. Internal walls would have separated the spaces used by the monks and lay brothers. A wall encircled the abbey and various secular buildings, enclosing an area of 11ha (27 acres).

Right: The southeast corner ruins of Tintern Abbey

TINTERN'S DEMISE

Edward II took refuge at Tintern for two nights in 1326. Tintern had been relatively untouched by the Welsh wars waged by his father, Edward I, but the Black Death of 1349 hampered recruitment of lay brothers, creating a labour shortage. The lands had to be let to tenant farmers. Further financial problems followed Welsh rebel leader Owain Glyndwr's uprising in the early 15th century.

Tintern was the wealthiest abbey in Wales but in 1536 it fell foul of Henry VIII's First Act of Suppression, designed to wrest power and wealth from the Church and cut ties with Rome. Tintern decayed into an ivy-covered ruin, visited from the mid-18th century onwards, when exploring Britain's wild and romantic places became popular. The picturesque ruins of Tintern were immortalized in a 1798 poem by Wordsworth, and in paintings by Turner.

Below: Ruins of Rievaulx Abbey in the North York Moors National Park

OTHER CISTERCIAN ABBEYS OF YORKSHIRE

Fountains Abbey and Rievaulx Abbey, both founded in 1132, were among the largest and richest in Britain. Abbots sat in Parliament and enjoyed immense political as well as spiritual power. Lay brothers mined lead and iron, with Rievaulx even producing cast iron. At one time Rievaulx was said to house 140 monks, as well as many lay brothers. In the 14th century these abbeys, too, were affected by the Black Death epidemic, and by Scottish raids, and were forced to lease out their granges. Rievaulx Abbey was eventually dissolved in 1538 and Fountains Abbey in 1539.

MIDDLE EAST

ABU SIMBEL

AMONG EGYPT'S BEST-KNOWN SIGHTS, THE SPECTACULAR ROCK-CUT TEMPLES OF ABU SIMBEL ARE LOCATED ABOUT 280KM (174 MILES) SOUTH OF ASWAN. THEIR CONSTRUCTION IS A TESTAMENT TO ONE OF ANCIENT EGYPT'S MOST AMBITIOUS BUILDERS.

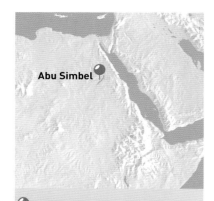

Abu Simbel

WHERE IS IT?
280km (174 miles) to the south of Aswan

WHEN TO VISIT
It is best to avoid visiting during late May–August as it is very hot—but these are also the least busy times

GENERAL INFO
The easiest way to get there is by air from Luxor/Cairo to Aswan, or as part of a Lake Nasser cruise. Convoys of buses and cars depart twice daily from Aswan. Visitors can also arrive by plane, at a specially constructed airfield for tourists

Doubtless the most famous of the seven temples Ramesses II built beyond ancient Egypt's southern border in Nubia, the Abu Simbel temples are the most recognizable rock-cut structures in Egypt. After being dedicated in the king's 24th year on the throne (c1255BC), the Great Temple, or Temple of Re-Horakhty, was damaged by an earthquake six years later, resulting in the loss of the upper portion of one of the king's statues. Despite restorations, the fallen colossus remains disjoined. After they fell into disuse, the temples became choked with sand, and in 1817 it took the might of Italian explorer and circus strongman Giovanni Battista Belzoni to make an attempt at clearing them.

KING AS GOD

The Abu Simbel temples honour a number of gods, but are specifically associated with deified forms of the king and his wife: the Great Temple with Ramesses and the Smaller Temple with his senior queen, Nefertari. Within the Great Temple, eight pillars in the form of colossal statues of the king as the god Osiris support the roof. The seated colossi of the deified Ramesses that front the temple each have individual names and may have been the object of religious devotion in their own right. Above the temple entrance, the king is shown with hands raised in adoration on both sides

Right: Façade of the relocated Great Temple of Abu Simbel

of a sculptured niche containing a symbolic writing of
one of his names: an animal's head, which represented
strength, User; the goddess Maat, who personified
truth; and the falcon-headed god Re: User-Maat-Re,
'strong is the Truth of Re'. Thus, the king literally
worships himself. Recorded on the exterior wall is an
account of the Battle of Kadesh, one of the earliest
documented military enounters—and which ended in
stalemate for Ramesses. Accompanying scenes give
a lively impression of the battlefield, but are biased in
showing an Egyptian victory.

SOLAR ALIGNMENT

Along the top of the temple's façade, it is possible to
discern a row of carved baboons. The animals' cries at
dawn were believed to be praise for the sun god, who
was one of the deities honoured at the temple. In the
sanctuary at the very rear, rock-cut statues depict the
deified king seated in the company of the major state
gods Re-Horakhty, Amun-Re and Ptah. The orientation
of the temple was designed to permit direct sunlight
to travel along its main axis and illuminate the group
twice a year. After the modern move of the temple, this
alignment was lost.

RESCUING RAMESSES

Abu Simbel was the focus of an international UNESCO
rescue campaign in the 1960s. In order to save the
temples from being submerged by the rising waters of
Lake Nasser, caused by the construction of the Aswan
High Dam, it was decided to move them to higher
ground. The temples were dismantled by cutting their
façades and decorated interiors into large blocks, then
reassembling them like a giant jigsaw puzzle inside a
modern concrete dome behind the cliff-face that can
be seen today. The operation cost $36 million.

Left: Seated colossi at the Great Temple of Ramesses II

**Right: Colossal statues depicting the king in the form of the
god Osiris, inside the Temple of Re-Horakhty**

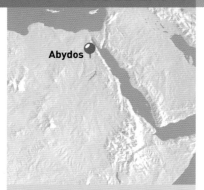

Abydos

WHERE IS IT?

145 km (90 miles) north of Luxor

WHEN TO VISIT

If you are averse to hot temperatures, it is best to avoid visiting during late May–August, but these are also the least busy times

GENERAL INFO

Some tours include Abydos on their itineraries, but it is easiest for independent travellers to take the three-hour trip on the Cairo train from Luxor to the local town, Balyana, and then make the short taxi journey to the archaeological sites

ABYDOS

ABYDOS WAS ONE OF THE MOST HALLOWED SITES FOR THE EGYPTIANS, BEING THE PRINCIPAL CULT CENTRE OF THE GOD OF THE DEAD, OSIRIS. THOUGH NOT OFTEN INCLUDED ON TOURIST ITINERARIES, IT BOASTS SOME OF THE MOST IMPRESSIVE TEMPLE REMAINS FROM PHARAONIC EGYPT.

Many Egyptians aspired to undertake a pilgrimage to Abydos, with tomb paintings and models frequently depicting boats used to make this sacred journey.

PILGRIMS AND PROCESSIONS

Countless pilgrims left cups, bowls, flasks and other pottery vessels with offerings for Osiris. These stained the desert surface red, giving rise to the

site's modern Arabic name, Umm el-Qaab—'Mother of Pots'. Numerous stelae and statues were also left to commemorate individuals and to allow them to magically participate in the major festival held at the site in honour of Osiris. This included processions of the god's statue from his temple to his supposed 'tomb', where the Egyptians believed the god had been buried after being murdered by his evil brother Seth. In fact, the tomb belonged to Djer, one of Egypt's earliest kings, whose burial place doubtless lent Abydos its special significance.

TEMPLES

Perhaps the most beautifully decorated temple in Egypt, the Temple of Seti I (c1280BC) is one of Egypt's hidden gems. It is unusual for its L-shaped plan and, despite having lost its outer pylons, contains a complex arrangement of rooms unlike any other Egyptian temple. Inside, architectural details, wall reliefs and even individual hieroglyphs are executed in the finest detail. One wall towards the rear of the temple shows Seti I and his son, the future Ramesses II, who completed the decoration of the structure in a somewhat more rushed style to that found elsewhere in the temple. Father and son stand before a list of royal names, honouring their royal ancestors. As well as highlighting a deep consciousness of Egypt's long dynastic history, the Abydos 'kings' list' provides a valuable resource for historians in reconstructing a chronological framework for Egyptian history.

MYSTERIOUS STRUCTURE

At the rear of the main temple lies the Osireon, a mysterious semi-subterranean structure approached through a long sloping corridor. The Osireon was designed to resemble a royal tomb, like those in the Valley of the Kings. Exceptionally, this 'dummy' tomb has a central island, surrounded by groundwater—representing the primeval ocean out of which the Egyptians believed life first emerged. The monolithic architecture of this temple resembles some of the earliest stonework used by the Egyptians, intentionally replicating its archaic style.

Above: The goddess Hathor gives life—symbolized by the ankh sign—to King Seti I

Left: Pots, the remains of pilgrims' offerings, still litter the site

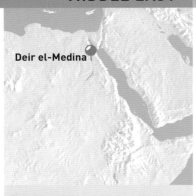

Deir el-Medina

WHERE IS IT?

On the west bank of the Nile, Luxor

WHEN TO VISIT

If you are averse to hot temperatures, it is best to avoid visiting during late May–August—but these are also the least busy times

GENERAL INFO

To get there you can either take a taxi from the east bank over the Nile bridge or take a passenger ferry from Luxor corniche to el-Gezira. Frequent ferries cross the river until late evening. The river can also be crossed by private motorboat. There are always taxis waiting at the ferry terminal to take visitors around the monuments

Right: Scene of the jackal-headed god Anubis attending the mummy of Senedjem, Tomb No. 1 in the Deir el-Medina necropolis

DEIR EL-MEDINA

THIS ARTIFICIAL DESERT SETTLEMENT IS ONE OF THE BEST PRESERVED IN EGYPT AND OFFERS AN UNPARALLELED INSIGHT INTO THE LIVES OF THE PEOPLE BEHIND THE CONSTRUCTION OF SOME OF EGYPT'S GREATEST ROYAL TOMBS.

Situated in a desolate bay in the Theban cliffs, the village of Deir el-Medina housed the builders of the royal tombs in the nearby Valley of the Kings during the New Kingdom (c1550BC–1069BC)—the 'servants of the Place of Truth'—along with their families. The seclusion of the village is probably more pronounced now than it was in antiquity, when a constant stream of supplies was delivered to the village. The path beaten by the workers' countless trips between the village and their workplace in the valley can still be traversed, giving the feeling of walking in the steps of the ancients.

VILLAGE LIFE

Living conditions within the settlement for the workmen and their families were cramped; the thick outer wall prevented significant expansion to adjust to fluctuations in the size of the workforce. The lower walls of around 70 houses remain and visitors can walk among the ancient streets and individual dwellings. Archaeologists have been able to ascribe individual ownership to many, using identifications known from inscribed sources. The wealth of written material from the site, mainly on scraps of limestone and potsherds, indicates an uncommonly high literacy rate among villagers. Combining these texts with archaeological data from Deir el-Medina provides historians with the richest source of information about the lives of the ancient Egyptians from a single site.

RELIGION AND WORSHIP

Beside the village proper lay the modest chapels of the workers' community, testifying to extensive religious practice at the site, hardly surprising for a community charged with creating the pharaoh's tomb. Several local gods were worshipped at the site, including the snake goddess Meretseger, the cow-headed goddess Hathor and Ptah, the patron god of craftsmen. Amenhotep I and his mother, Queen Ahmose-Nefertari, were accorded particular importance as both the founders and the patrons of the village. Numerous local festivals took place around the chapels, at which divine statues were carried aloft and their movements—or the movements of the priests carrying them—were interpreted to give answers to questions posed of the gods.

TOMBS OF THE TOMB-BUILDERS

The artisans, with skills acquired from work on royal projects, were able to create their own beautifully decorated tombs to the west of the village. While only a fraction of the size of the nearby tombs of their royal masters, the workmen's burial places are brightly coloured and display a striking individuality in their craftsmanship. Many tombs were discovered intact, offering more information about the villagers' lives and beliefs. Several included small pyramids atop their superstructures, ultimately aping much earlier royal designs.

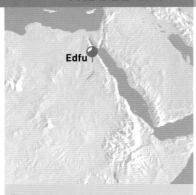

Edfu

EDFU

DEDICATED TO THE FALCON-HEADED GOD HORUS, THE PTOLEMAIC TEMPLE
OF EDFU IS THE MOST COMPLETELY PRESERVED IN EGYPT.

Nestled within the modern town of Edfu, the Temple
of Horus is typical of Graeco-Roman maintenance of
traditional forms in Egyptian religious architecture.
Under the Ptolemies, reconstruction and
embellishment was undertaken at many temple sites
throughout Egypt, and Edfu replaced a much earlier
shrine at the same site.

CONSTRUCTION AT EDFU

Building work at Edfu began in 237BC under Ptolemy
III and, after various phases of construction and

enlargement, decoration was completed in 57BC. As
an act of piety par excellence, the boom in temple
construction was designed to consolidate and
legitimize the Greek dynasty's claim to Egypt's ancient
kingship. Throughout the temple the Ptolemies are
depicted in full Egyptian regalia, carrying out rituals
that by the time they were carved were already several
millennia old.

SACRED ATMOSPHERE

From the outer pylon—the gateway that formed the

Right: Columned pronaos of the temple

**Far right: The best preserved of a
pair of granite statues of the falcon
god Horus at the entrance to the
temple**

façade of most Egyptian temples—the visitor first enters the colonnaded forecourt, then moves into the densely-pillared pronaos before reaching the inner sanctum of the god's domain. Proceeding towards the sanctuary at the rear of the temple, the floor level rises and the ceiling lowers until the heart of the temple is reached. Light levels are controlled by slits, and though the effect of the originally brightly painted walls is lost, the feeling of this enclosed space evokes a sense of being one of the few priests privileged to approach the god's statue directly. It would have been kept within the monolithic polished black stone shrine, or naos, dedicated by Egypt's last native king, Nectanebo II (360–343BC), and retained by later Ptolemaic builders.

HORUS, LIVING GOD OF THE TEMPLE

The Egyptians' veneration of sacred animals is well known, and usually focused on a single member of one species. At Edfu, the god Horus was thought to be incarnate in a sacred falcon. The god is shown as a falcon-headed man in reliefs throughout the temple and a pair of colossal granite falcons positioned at the temple's gateways depict him in his full avian guise. In addition to a statue, made of precious metal and kept in the sanctuary, a specially bred living falcon was selected to represent the god on earth. Once chosen, the sacred bird was crowned, then taken to the bridge between the wings of the front pylon of the temple—the so-called Balcony of the Falcon—and ceremonially presented to onlookers below.

TEMPLE RITUAL

Detailed scenes and inscriptions on the temple's walls describe other rituals that were carried out to honour the god. In addition to a daily ritual to 'wake' and 'feed' the god (in the form of his statue), special rites included priestly processions of the statue to celebrate the New Year by exposing it to the regenerating rays of the sun on the temple's roof, and a dramatic ritual which re-enacted the victory of Horus over his enemy Seth, represented as a speared hippopotamus.

● MORE HORUS RITUAL

One of the most widely-celebrated rituals was the 'marriage' of Horus and the cow-headed goddess Hathor, which involved a processional journey of the god's statue from Edfu to Dendera, another impressive Ptolemaic temple, although not as well preserved as Edfu, a distance of 180km (112 miles) away.

GIZA

SITUATED ON THE GIZA PLATEAU, AT THE EDGE OF THE MODERN CAIRO SPRAWL, THESE MAN-MADE MOUNTAINS ARE THE SOLE SURVIVING MEMBER OF THE SEVEN WONDERS OF THE ANCIENT WORLD. TOGETHER WITH THE GREAT SPHINX, THE PYRAMIDS ARE BREATHTAKING ICONS OF ANCIENT EGYPT.

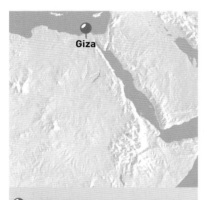

Giza

WHERE IS IT?

At the end of Pyramid Road, 18km (11 miles) southwest of central Cairo

WHEN TO VISIT

The site is open to visitors daily 7–7.30 and the pyramids are open in rotation, 8.30–4 daily. It is best to avoid visiting during late May–August when it is very hot—but these are also the least busy times

GENERAL INFO

A short taxi ride from most city-centre hotels and hostels

Giza's three pyramids represent the monumental tombs of three successive generations. Khufu (c2560BC) was the first to build his pyramid at the site. At 146.6m (481ft) tall, Khufu's Great Pyramid is Egypt's largest and until the 14th century AD was the tallest building in the world, when Lincoln Cathedral's spire outdid it. Each side of the base originally measured 231m (756ft), and in total the pyramid contains over 2.3 million blocks. During the Middle Ages, it formed a convenient quarry of ready-dressed blocks, as its outer layer of stone was stripped to build medieval Cairo. The pyramid has been open since antiquity, but admission is now by limited numbers to regulate humidity inside. The interior highlights the builders' precision: the steeply sloping entrance passage opens out into the spectacular, corbelled Grand Gallery, which in turn leads to the burial chamber. Lined with granite brought from quarries at Aswan, almost 800km (497 miles) up the Nile, the room still contains the king's sarcophagus. The fact that the sarcophagus is 2.5cm (1in) wider than the entrance to the room indicates that it was installed during construction.

Right: Face of the Great Sphinx, with the Pyramid of Khafre

Next spread: The pyramids in a remote desert location

A FAMILY AFFAIR

Smaller, and with a simpler interior, Khafre's pyramid still retains some of its original casing of fine white limestone from the nearby quarries at Tura. Khufu's grandson, Menkaure, was the last king to build at Giza, employing granite blocks to face the lower courses of his pyramid, the smallest of the three. The entrance owes its scarred appearance to the use of dynamite by 19th-century treasure-seekers. Menkaure's sarcophagus was lost at sea, when the ship carrying it sank.

LOCATION, LOCATION

Contrary to popular belief, the Pyramids do not stand
alone in the desert. They are surrounded by numerous
tombs of members of the royal court, buried next to
their royal overlord. Temples attached to the pyramids
allowed offerings to be made to the dead king.
Although much ruined, their black basalt pavements
can still be seen today. Covered causeways originally
connected these with similar structures near the river.
Despite radical theories about alien involvement in
their construction, settlement remains on the Giza
plateau confirm the vast human organization required
for such projects.

THE GREAT SPHINX

With the body of a lion and the head of a king—either
Khufu or Khafre—the Great Sphinx at Giza is the
largest man-made sculpture in the world. At 73.5m
(241ft) in length and over 20m (66ft) high, it is hardly
surprising that even long after its construction the
Sphinx itself was venerated as a god, as shown
by a series of chapels that cluster around it. The
monumental slab, or stela, between the paws of the
Sphinx records how a young prince named Tuthmosis
was hunting in the desert at Giza one day and stopped
to sleep in the shade of the monument. The prince
dreamt that the Sphinx spoke to him, asking him to
remove the windblown sand that covered its body. In
return, the Sphinx would make the prince Pharaoh.
The stela is damaged and the ending of its inscription
lost, but the fact the stela was dedicated by King
Tuthmosis IV shows the Sphinx to have been true to its
word. Weathering has afflicted the monument since
its construction, and its stonework has undergone
extensive restoration until modern times.

Left: Aerial view of the Giza plateau

**Right: The so-called 'Dream Stela' between the paws of the
Great Sphinx**

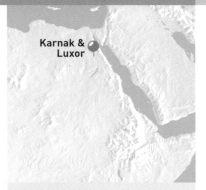

Karnak &
Luxor

WHERE IS IT?
Both are on the east bank of the
Nile, Luxor, the latter in the central
part of town opposite the ferry dock

WHEN TO VISIT
Avoid visiting during late May–
August when it is at its hottest—but
these are the least busy times

GENERAL INFO
Against the dramatic backdrop of
megalithic statues and obelisks, a
sound and light show takes place
at Karnak and Luxor three times
each night

KARNAK AND LUXOR

LOCATED AT THE HEART OF ANCIENT THEBES, KARNAK AND LUXOR
TOGETHER FORM ONE OF THE LARGEST RELIGIOUS COMPLEXES IN THE
WORLD AND TELL A HISTORY IN STONE OF EGYPT'S GREATEST KINGS. THE
TEMPLES SERVED AS THE HOMES OF THE GODS ON EARTH AND WERE THE
SUBJECT OF CONSTANT RENOVATION AND EXPANSION.

The vast complex celebrated the cult of the state-
god Amun-Re and his divine wife and child, Mut and
Khonsu, in addition to other divinities. Each had their
own temple or chapel within the precincts of Karnak.
The importance of Amun and his temple had grown
steadily from the early Middle Kingdom (c2000BC),
well into the Late Period (664–3BC). Building work
was greatest during the New Kingdom (c1550–
1269BC) at the height of Egypt's military dominance
of neighbouring lands, and the spoils of successful
campaigns brought wealth that expanded the complex.
Amun had originally been a locally revered deity in
the Theban region, but grew in stature to become
pre-eminent among the gods, ensuring Egypt's
imperial ambitions.

PYLONS AND PROCESSIONS

Karnak is built on two main axes. The earliest
stretches from east to west and includes the
spectacular columned Hypostyle Hall, constructed and
decorated by Seti I and his son Ramesses II. A later
branch was added stretching towards the Temple of

**Left: Avenue of sphinxes constructed by Egypt's last native
dynasty leading towards Luxor**

**Right: Colossal statue built by Ramesses II outside Karnak
temple, and later reinscribed by subsequent kings**

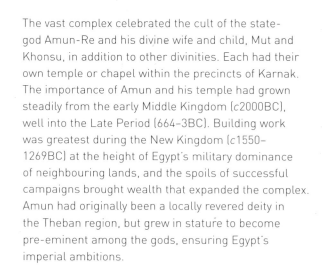

Mut in the south. Karnak grew organically over time, with new building work being undertaken by each king. Each section or courtyard within the temples was fronted by stone towers, called pylons, to maintain the sanctity of events within from the uninitiated outside. Ironically, the front (or first) pylon was the last to be built, and is unfinished; the mud-brick ramps used in its construction can still be seen around its base. Originally, the pylons were embellished with flagstaffs, obelisks and colossal statues, a few of which remain to be seen today. The primary purpose of the temple was as a home for the god, and a suitable setting for rites in his honour. Processional avenues of sphinxes connected the main temple with outlying shrines, which housed other deities. The holiest part of the temple was the sanctuary at the rear. The present structure to house the god's statue was built by the Macedonian king Philip Arrhidaeus around 320BC but replicates in form and decoration one constructed under Tuthmosis III, over a millennium earlier.

CACHETTE

Perhaps the most spectacular discovery at the site came in 1903, when French Egyptologist Georges Legrain uncovered the first of what turned out to be several thousand statues, stelae and bronze votive offerings. More recently, a similar though much smaller cache was found at Luxor. Both Karnak and Luxor would originally have been filled with statues, dedicated by both kings and non-royal persons to ensure a perpetual presence in the temple. Though few remain in situ, these caches represent the pious actions of priests at the temples, in collecting and burying ritual objects in sacred ground.

TEMPLE STAFF

A vast clergy, mostly employed in rotation, was required in order to perform the daily rituals to appease the god. One of the most common Egyptian words for priest means pure. The temple staff were required to wash themselves, probably in Karnak's sacred lake to the

south of the sanctuary, before going about their work. Additionally, the priesthood undertook to chant liturgy, copy documents in the temple library, carry the god's statue when it travelled in procession and to maintain the temple building generally. Many of these individuals are attested by their names and titles on a vast number of commemorative statuettes they left at the site.

POWER AND INFLUENCE

In addition to its religious significance, Karnak was also a major land-owning institution, with considerable economic power. An army of scribes would have administered the temple's holdings. Their ranks were headed by a single individual known as the First Prophet (or High Priest) of Amun, who was also the chief ritualist at the temple. With such influence, it is little wonder that by the end of the New Kingdom (c1069BC) the High Priest of Amun had given himself the title of 'king'. Karnak's highest office did not always remain male-dominated. By the time of the Nubian 25th Dynasty (c747–656BC), Thebes was under the jurisdiction of the God's Wife of Amun—a form of ritual spouse for the deity—and was administered by her High Steward. The title of God's Wife was usually held by royal daughters and was of central political importance in controlling the Theban region.

SOUTHERN EXPANSION

A little to the south of Karnak, Luxor derives its name from the Arabic meaning the 'palaces', based on a misconception about the original function of its ruins. The present temple honoured a regenerative form of the god Amun and is largely the work of one of Egypt's greatest builders, Amenhotep III. It was created to accommodate the annual Opet festival, which celebrated royal and divine fertility and regeneration. Like many ancient Egyptian structures, Luxor had several later functions: first as a military garrison in Roman times, then subsequently the first court was used as the site of the mosque of Abu el-Haggag, which can still be seen today.

Above: Columns and architraves at the rear of Karnak, with remains of their original painted decoration

Right: Colonnade of Luxor, fronted by colossi of Ramesses II

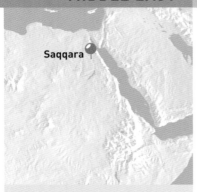

Saqqara

WHERE IS IT?

About an hour's drive from central Cairo. It is a mainstay of most tour stops

WHEN TO VISIT

If you are averse to hot temperatures, it is best to avoid visiting during late May–August— but these are also the least busy times

GENERAL INFO

The site opens daily 8–4

SAQQARA

ABOUT 40KM (25 MILES) SOUTH OF MODERN CAIRO, SAQQARA SERVED AS THE MAIN NECROPOLIS FOR EGYPT'S CAPITAL, MEMPHIS, AND REMAINED IMPORTANT THROUGHOUT THE PHARAONIC PERIOD AND BEYOND. ITS CONTINUED AND INTENSE USE IS REFLECTED IN THE WEALTH OF ARCHAEOLOGICAL FINDS FROM THE SITE.

Today, as in ancient times, the focal point at Saqqara is the complex of buildings that surrounds the Step Pyramid—the world's earliest major stone building and the earliest pyramid in Egypt. Built for King Djoser around 2650BC, it set the trend for Egyptian pyramid construction. Before Djoser, the traditional form of royal sepulchre was the mud-brick mastaba tomb— a low, rectangular structure that takes its name from the Arabic word for bench. Northern Saqqara was the chosen spot for a large number of these tombs long before Djoser came to the throne, and they must have dominated the desert horizon when viewed from nearby Memphis. By piling a series of mastaba tombs one on top of the other, a six-stepped pyramid was formed.

MASTER BUILDER

The Egyptians themselves credited the innovations of the Step Pyramid to a man named Imhotep. Known from contemporary sources, his titles conveniently fit the modern job description of architect—the first known to history. Long after his death, Imhotep was revered as a god of wisdom and medicine, and Saqqara became a centre for his worship. A museum at the site is named after Imhotep and celebrates his achievement and legacy. Exhibits describe Saqqara's history through a series of fascinating objects discovered at the site.

ETERNITY IN STONE

Djoser's complex owes much of its present appearance to the work of architect and Egyptologist Jean-Philippe Lauer. The Frenchman spent decades carefully sorting through thousands of scattered blocks around the Step Pyramid and succeeded in reconstructing many of the structures within the complex. These included 'dummy' limestone versions of buildings originally made of less durable materials. These solid facsimiles represent the various cultic palaces and chapels used by the king for the celebration of his *heb-sed*, or jubilee festival, after 30 years on the throne. A replica of the king's statue— the original is in Cairo Museum—can be viewed in its sealed *serdab*, or statue-chamber, peering out through a small aperture to the ceremonies outside. Rendered in stone, this celebration of royal rejuvenation was thought to continue for eternity. Entering the restored façade of the enclosure wall, visitors get a vivid impression of the complex as it might have originally appeared. In their elegance and simplicity, the lines of Egypt's earliest monumental forms echo architectural trends seen much later in classical Greece.

TOMBS WITH A VIEW

Djoser and his architect set a trend. Saqqara is the site of no fewer than 14 pyramids. Particularly noteworthy are the later monuments of Unas and Teti that, though the pyramids themselves are little more than mounds

Top right: Mummified falcon, inside a pottery coffin

Right: The six-stepped pyramid of King Djoser, the world's first major stone monument

of rubble, contain rooms whose walls are completely covered in *Pyramid Texts*—the first attested religious literature in the world. As royal pyramids decreased in size and quality, so the tombs of non-royal officials increased in both architectural complexity and the extent of their decoration. Contemporary with Unas and Teti's pyramids, large multi-roomed mastabas of high officials such as Mereruka, Kagemni and Ptahhotep are decorated with lively scenes depicting idealized episodes from the life of the tomb owner. These monuments were considered ancient by the time of Tutankhamun, and the site continued to inspire later members of the elite to build their tombs in close proximity to royal ones. Throughout Egyptian history, Saqqara would truly have been a city of the dead, as attested by ancient graffiti recording visits by tourists.

SACRED ANIMALS

Saqqara continued to be an important religious site into the Late Period (c664–32BC). An entire necropolis flourished at Saqqara into Roman times for sacred animals, with a series of temples serving the cults of various gods and their associated divine fauna. Millions of animals were bred, killed and then mummified before being sold to pilgrims, to be buried in further underground galleries as votive offerings to the gods.

HOLY COW

The cult of the Apis bull, which honoured a single animal selected for its particular markings believed to embody the spirit of the god Ptah, probably has its origins at the beginning of Egyptian history. From the New Kingdom (c1550–1069BC), each deceased bull was buried in the subterranean complex known as the Serapeum, which still contains the monolithic sarcophagi of many.

VALLEY OF THE KINGS

ON THE WEST BANK OF ANCIENT THEBES, OPPOSITE THE GREAT TEMPLES OF KARNAK AND LUXOR, THE VALLEY WAS THE FAVOURED LOCATION FOR THE 'SECRET' TOMBS OF SOME OF EGYPT'S MOST FAMOUS RULERS.

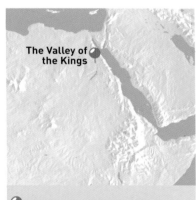

The Valley of the Kings

WHERE IS IT?
On the west bank of the Nile, Luxor

WHEN TO VISIT
Avoid visiting during late May–August when it is very hot—but these are the least busy times

GENERAL INFO
Frequent ferries cross the river until late evening. The river can also be crossed by private motorboat. There are always taxis waiting at the ferry terminal to take visitors around the monuments

Beneath the towering natural pyramid of the Theban mountain (the *Qurn*, or 'horn' in Arabic) stretches a landscape that was in use throughout Egypt's New Kingdom (*c*1550–1069BC) and contains the tombs of some of Egypt's greatest kings. This mountain peak was sacred to the snake goddess Meretseger, whose name means 'she who loves silence'. Arriving early in the morning, visitors are often struck by the silence in the valley, and a feeling of solitude.

HIGHLIGHTS

Each tomb has a Kings' Valley (KV) number, depending on its date of discovery, and many are open and easily accessible. Among the most impressive tombs is the cliff-tomb of Tuthmosis III (KV 34) with its burial chamber decorated with stick figure wall paintings, made to resemble a large unrolled papyrus. KV 8 (Merenptah) and K14 (begun by Queen Tawosret and adapted by Setnakht) have retained many of their coloured scenes of mythological content. KV 5 is the largest in the valley and is the subject of ongoing investigation. While most royal children were buried in the nearby Valley of the Queens, Ramesses II (*r*1279–1213BC) had this elaborate mausoleum constructed for his extensive family.

SECRETS AND LIES

A supposed advantage of the valley compared to previous royal cemeteries was its secrecy. Royal tombs and the temples that celebrated the cults of the dead rulers were built separately, and one architect even boasted that he constructed his king's tomb 'with no one seeing, no one hearing'. Tombs stocked with precious grave goods were, however, difficult secrets to keep. Not long after they received their occupants, most major royal tombs were robbed. Dramatic accounts of robbers' trials survive, recounting their confessions under torture. The discovery of a number of caches of royal mummies, stripped of their precious grave goods, further attests to the widespread practice of tomb violation.

THE GOLDEN BOY

Worldwide attention came to the valley in 1922, with the discovery of the tomb of the boy king Tutankhamun (r1336–1327BC). Though a relatively minor ruler, the quality and quantity of his grave goods were astonishing. Crammed into a tiny tomb, his burial was modest by the standards of most of Egypt's kings; his tomb probably belonged to an official before being converted for the king's use after his untimely death at a young age. Consequently the space is small and visitor numbers are limited. Only the burial chamber is decorated and, although not as spectacular as many later royal tombs in the valley, still contains the king's mummy. Unlike most of the valley's royal occupants, who are now displayed in the Egyptian Museum in Cairo, one can gaze on the face of Tutankhamun in his own tomb.

Left: The decorated burial chamber of Tutankhamun, which still contains the king's mummy

Right: Pendant of Tutankhamun

Next spread: The Temple of the Hatshepsut

VALLEY OF THE QUEENS

Royal sons, wives and other royal family members were not interred in the Valley of the Kings, but in one nearby, known today as the Valley of the Queens. It contains some of the most finely painted tombs in Egypt, including that of Nefertari, wife of Ramesses II. The tomb's bright colours are particularly striking after having been extensively restored, but their fragility has necessitated extremely limited numbers of tourists being permitted to enter.

Persepolis

WHERE IS IT?

Modern Takht-e Jamshid, Fars province, 72.5km (45 miles) northeast of Shiraz, Iran

WHEN TO VISIT

Spring or autumn

GENERAL INFO

The site is accessible by road from Shiraz, and is 43.5km (27 miles) from the earlier Persian capital, Pasargadae

PERSEPOLIS

THIRTEEN COLUMNS OF THE APADANA STILL FORLORNLY STANDING ATTEST TO THE FORMER GRANDEUR OF THE ANCIENT PERSIAN CAPITAL, PERSEPOLIS, WANTONLY TORCHED BY ALEXANDER THE GREAT IN 330BC. ALEXANDER'S CONFLAGRATION DESTROYED THE PRINCIPAL BUILDINGS, BUT IRONICALLY, BY BAKING THEM, IT PRESERVED AN INVALUABLE ARCHIVE OF CLAY CUNEIFORM TABLETS.

This archive sheds great light on the administrative life of Persepolis, the Achaemenid seat of government. The city was founded around 518BC by the second Persian king, Darius the Great, and the main buildings were completed by his successors, Xerxes and Artaxerxes I, though later kings also built palaces here. The last kings of the Achaemenid dynasty were buried in rock-cut tombs, in the Kuh-i Rahmat Mountain overlooking the city. Part of the mountain was cut away and consolidated to create a terrace on which the city's principal buildings were constructed. This was surrounded by a wall, 10m (33ft) thick, with many

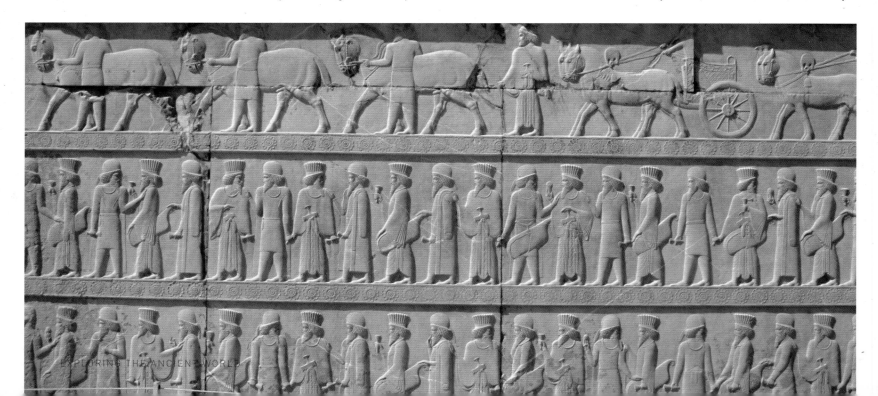

towers. A magnificent stairway led up to the platform where the visitor had first to pass through Xerxes' Gate of All the Nations, an imposing chamber whose three gateways were protected by monumental guardian figures of bulls and man-headed bulls.

PUBLIC MAGNIFICENCE

Darius wished Persepolis to display the splendour of the Persian Empire through festivals, ceremonies and receptions held in its magnificent buildings, particularly the Apadana, the Audience Hall that dominated the northern end of the terrace. This originally had 72 massive stone columns, with beautiful bell-shaped bases and capitals in the form of addorsed bulls, supporting a roof of cedar beams. To its east Xerxes constructed the Throne Hall, with 100 columns, to host receptions for representatives of the empire's subject nations. A procession of delegations from 23 of these is depicted on the slabs decorating the great staircases that led up to the Apadana. They are shown in national costumes, from barefooted Indians in dhotis and headbands to Scythians in tunics, trousers, boots and pointed caps. Each brings tribute typical of their region: cattle, horses and camels, gold and silver vessels and jewellery, bottles of perfume, fine textiles, weapons and whole tusks of ivory. These were deposited in the Treasury, a large building constructed by Darius, greatly extended by Xerxes, and finally over-spilling its contents into the Throne Hall behind which it lay. When Alexander sacked the city, he carried off from here 5,000 camel-loads and 20,000 mule-loads of treasure.

PRIVATE SPLENDOUR

Behind these public buildings lay the palaces constructed by the individual kings and the enormous L-shaped harem that housed the royal women and their households. The stairs approaching these and other buildings were also decorated with figures, court officials and guards, but also servants bearing covered dishes of food. The great doorways to many

of the buildings were carved with figures of the king: Darius on his throne, with Xerxes standing behind him, beneath the symbol of the Persian supreme deity, Ahura-Mazda; or the king in combat with a lion or a monster, a traditonal Near Eastern theme stretching back more than 2,000 years.

Above: Detail of the Xerxes' gate

Left: Apadana staircase

MASADA

THE DESERT FORTRESS OF HEROD THE GREAT CAPTURED BY
ROMAN FORCES DURING THE JEWISH REVOLT IS, NEXT TO
JERUSALEM, THE MOST POPULAR DESTINATION OF JEWISH
VISITORS TO ISRAEL.

WHERE IS IT?
At the southwest tip of the Dead
Sea in Israel

GENERAL INFO
Access can be made from the
western side via the Roman
siege ramp, or via cable car from
the east where there are visitor
facilities

The fortress of Masada is situated on an outcrop
looking over the Dead Sea, and is surrounded by steep
precipices. It became famous during the Jewish Revolt
for its siege cAD72 described by the Jewish historian
Josephus. It was reported that the garrison committed
suicide rather than fall into the hands of Rome.

HERODIAN PALACE
A spectacular royal palace was created by Herod the
Great (c74–4BC) at the northern end of the outcrop
on a series of three terraces. He wanted something
to compare with the palaces of the Hellenistic world
at Vergina in Macedonia, Alexandria and Pergamom.
Classical architecture and wall paintings emulating
exotic marble panels show that Herod was keen to
reflect the cultured taste of Rome. Herod constructed
a further palace complex at Jericho just to the north of
the Dead Sea.

THE SYNAGOGUE
This rectangular structure was found adjacent to
the western wall of the fortress. A series of benches
ran round the inside of the walls, and it was clearly
roofed by the presence of internal columns. The
earliest phase seems to be contemporary with the
Royal Palace, but the synagogue appears to have been
adapted at the time of the Jewish Revolt. The function
of the building may be confirmed by the discovery of a
fragment from the Book of the Law (Deuteronomy).

THE STOREHOUSES
The palace complex, and later the fortress, were
supplied from massive storehouse complexes. These
had areas containing amphorae for olive oil and wine,
as well as areas for grain. The structures seem to
have been destroyed by fire around the time of the
Roman siege.

ROMAN FORTIFICATIONS
After the fall of Jerusalem the Roman General Flavius

BYZANTINE CHURCH

Occupation continued after the Roman sack of the fortress. A small garrison seems to have occupied the site. In Late Antiquity a Byzantine church was built on the summit. This was decorated with a mosaic, probably made in the 5th century AD, which included hanging grapes.

Left: The fortress of Masada

Silva marched on Masada. His men constructed an encircling wall strengthened by a series of forts; one of the most accessible is adjacent to the car park near the cable-car station. Silva's command seems to have been located immediately opposite the palace on the western side. A massive siege ramp was constructed from the western side; pieces of original wood can still be seen protruding from the earthwork. An artillery bastion protected this, where catapults and other field-weapons could be used to fire on any defenders.

BATHS

An example of the taste for Roman culture is reflected in the Roman bathing complex complete with hot-rooms, which was constructed just to the south of the Royal Palace. Traces of the wall painting survived, as well as the mosaic floors. Fragments of the sculptural reliefs showing rosettes were reused during the Jewish Revolt.

Right: The bathhouse

JERASH

IMPRESSIVE JERASH REMAINS IN EXCEPTIONAL CONDITION, AND IS CONSIDERED ONE OF THE LARGEST AND BEST-PRESERVED CLASSICAL CITIES IN THE WORLD. EXCAVATIONS AT THIS SETTING BEGAN IN THE 1920S AND CONTINUE TODAY.

Jerash

WHERE IS IT?
50km (31 miles) north of Amman, Jordan

GENERAL INFO
www.visitjordan.com
www.jerashchariots.com
The Jerash Festival takes place in July

Jerash, the ancient city of Gerasa, was probably established in the Hellenistic period as part of the Decapolis (or community of Ten Cities) largely, but not completely, to the east of the River Jordan. Its original name, Antiochia on the Chrysorhoas, suggests that it may have been founded by one of the rulers with the name Antiochus. The city then formed part of the Roman province of Syria under its transfer to Arabia from AD105–106. Its wealth depended on the caravan routes eastwards.

TEMPLE OF ZEUS

The Temple of Zeus was constructed in AD22–43. The original benefactor was one Zabdion, son of Aristomachos, priest of Tiberius Caesar. The temple may have been rebuilt in the Antonine period. Inscriptions mention the presence of temple-slaves, and there has been a suggestion that the cult was perhaps similar to that of Baal found elsewhere in the Near East.

TEMPLE OF ARTEMIS

Artemis was the patron deity of the city. The temple appears to have been constructed in the middle of the 2nd century AD in the Antonine period. The temple used the Corinthian order of architecture.

FORUM

This public space was elliptical in shape and surrounded by rows of columns. An inscription shows that a major public building was added to this area under the emperor Nero in AD66. One of the main colonnaded streets, now known as the Via Antoniniana, leads east from it. On the north side of this street was the *macellum* or meat market. A monumental tetrapylon was erected where this main north-to-south street meets the main east-to-west street.

THE THEATRE AND ODEION

The south theatre was constructed during the reign of the emperor Domitian (AD81–96). The Odeion (or north

theatre) was a concert hall constructed AD165–166 during the co-regency of Marcus Aurelius and Lucius Verus. The original structure may have been roofed. The Odeion was further developed in the 3rd century during the reign of Alexander Severus. Inscriptions from the lower seating area show that the seating was divided into sections relating to the city tribes; one of the tribes is named after the emperor Hadrian. Jerash was also equipped with public bathhouses reflecting the way that the local population had adopted Roman customs.

BYZANTINE CHURCHES

Jerash became a major centre for Christianity in late antiquity and some 12 churches have been identified in the city. These date from the early 5th century AD. Among the largest was the basilica of St. Theodore dating from the end of the 5th century.

TRIUMPHAL ARCH

This freestanding structure (as above) was placed outside the area of the city to the south, next to the hippodrome, and was presumably intended for ceremonial purposes. The dedicatory inscription shows that it was dedicated in AD129–130. This corresponds with the journey of Hadrian from Antioch in Syria to Egypt during 130; during the trip he went through Jerash and the city of Jerusalem.

Left: The forum, also known as the oval plaza

PETRA

TWO THOUSAND YEARS AGO, PETRA STOOD AT A CROSSROADS
IN THE ANCIENT NEAR EAST. CAMEL CARAVANS PASSED
THROUGH, LOADED WITH SPICES, TEXTILES AND INCENSE
FROM DISTANT REGIONS, AND THROUGH SUCH COMMERCE,
THE CITY FLOURISHED.

Petra

WHERE IS IT?
226km (140 miles) southwest of
Amman, Jordan

WHEN TO VISIT
Winter, as summer temperatures
in Jordan can reach 48°C (118°F)

GENERAL INFO
You can travel by public minibus
or 'service' taxi from Amman bus
station to Wadi Mosa. Take plenty
of water, as walking the site is
thirsty work

Today, visitors to this 'Rose-red city, half as old as
time', as it was described by English poet J. W.
Burgon, come upon this remarkable ancient city
through a narrow gorge (Al-siq). At the end of the siq,
the passage opens up to reveal the first of Petra's
wonders, the Treasury.

OASIS IN THE DESERT

Petra's history and provenance are almost as colourful
as its weather-worn and human-hewn rock faces. It
was first established sometime around the 6th century
BC by the Nabataean Arabs, a nomadic tribe who
settled in the area, initially in tents.

Over the centuries, these patient and skilled people
created an oasis in the desert by the careful control of the river, springs and natural rainwater cycle,
using dams and irrigation systems. At the same time,
they chiselled the sandstone cliffs into the form of
freestanding temples and nearly 3,000 rock-cut tombs,
dwellings, banquet halls, altars and niches. Not only
were these structures elaborately carved, but they
were also covered with stucco and brightly painted.

At its height, around AD50, the city and its environs
boasted as many as 20,000 residents and the city was
a busy commercial crossroads on the trade routes
across the desert.

Right: Detail of the magnificent Treasury

THE TREASURY

The Treasury (Al-Khazneh) is an awe-inspiring sight as you emerge from the gorge leading into Petra. The façade, 30m (98ft) wide and 43m (141ft) high, is carved out of the sheer, pink rock face. It was built in the early 1st century as the tomb of an important Nabataean king and represents a pinnacle of the engineering genius of these ancient people. Its design is more classical than typically Nabataean, reflecting the growth of the Roman Empire and its growing influence on the Nabataean society of the time. Early 19th-century visitors to Petra believed the urn that tops the Treasury's façade contained treasures of a dead pharaoh and took pot shots at it in the hope of dislodging it.

THE ROMANS ARRIVE

For centuries Petra thrived in its remote valley, the ruling city of a rich, independent kingdom. But 2,414km (1,500 miles) to the west, another superpower was gathering size and strength. Rome, with its great wealth and hunger for new territory, as well as a seemingly invincible army, looked longingly towards the ancient Near East. When the empire began expanding eastward, the seizure of Petra was only a matter of time. In AD106 Emperor Trajan laid claim to all of Nabataea, calling his prize Arabia Petraea.

Once the kingdom of Nabataea was annexed, all Mediterranean trade fell under Roman imperial control. The new province also served as a staging post for campaigns against Parthia, a hostile Iranian kingdom further to the east. The takeover appears to have been bloodless, and life for ordinary Nabataeans probably went on much as before. Sheltered by Rome's might, trade routes were safer, and—at least for a while—caravans still stopped at Petra. For the next three centuries, the fate of the desert city would be tied to the fate of Rome.

EARTHQUAKE OF AD363

Many of the free-standing columns that were built by the Nabataeans during their tenure under the Roman empire were destroyed by earthquakes, particularly the mega-quake that seems to have struck the region in AD363. Records from the time suggest that half the city was destroyed, and archaeologists confirm considerable damage to the massive Nabataean-built, Roman-style amphitheatre, which could seat 3,000 people. It is still impressive today, so one can only imagine its former glory.

A good deal of the city's major temples (including the Qasr al-Bint) and colonnaded streets were also damaged but, even worse, the earthquake disrupted the water supply system, which was crucial to the

Left: Detail of the elaborate carved buildings that were chiselled into the pink rock face

survival of such a city in the desert. An economically healthy Petra might have rebounded, but changes in trade routes with the rise of Palmyra had already taken their toll on the city's financial viability. By AD363, Petra had lost the means to rebuild itself.

CITY WITH AN AFTERLIFE

Despite the earthquake damage and ravages of time, Petra still holds so much to awe the visitor. Ideally, you need at least four or five days to really explore the city. There are literally hundreds of intricate rock-cut tombs. Unlike the houses, which were probably made of mud, the tombs were carved to last into the afterlife, and 500 have survived, empty but mysterious as you file past their dark openings. There are obelisks, temples, sacrificial altars and colonnaded streets, and high above, overlooking the valley, is the impressive Al-Deir Monastery—up a flight of 800 rock cut steps. Within the site there are also two museums: the Petra Archaeological Museum and the Petra Nabataean Museum, both of which display finds from excavations in the Petra region and provide an insight into the city's past civilizations and sudden fall into decline.

Above: Nabataean tombs at the UNESCO World Heritage Site

Previous spread: Ravaged by earthquakes, the ruins of Petra are still awe inspiring

Leptis Magna

LEPTIS MAGNA

THIS WELL-PRESERVED ROMAN CITY IN NORTH AFRICA WAS ONCE THE HOME OF THE ROMAN EMPEROR SEPTIMIUS SEVERUS.

WHERE IS IT?
In western Libya, District of Khoms

GENERAL INFO
For further information see whc.unesco.org/en/list/183/; www.alnpete.co.uk/lepcis/

Leptis Magna was a major harbour-city on the north coast of Africa in the area known as Tripolitania. There is evidence for Punic occupation, but the city became important in the Roman period, becoming a formal colony in the early 2nd century AD. The city's wealth was partially built on the export of olive oil.

THE THEATRE

The theatre was constructed during the reign of the Roman emperor Augustus in 1–2AD due to the benefaction of Annobal Tapapius Rufus (the name reflecting the Punic origins of the inhabitants). Although the lowest section of seating was cut into a hillside, most of the seats rest on an artificial substructure. The theatre was provided with a dramatic stage backdrop, some three storeys high. Behind the theatre stood a sanctuary linked to the Roman imperial cult. The city also had a separate amphitheatre, perhaps seating some 16,000 people and in use by AD56, where gladiatorial shows and animal hunts could be presented.

MARKET AND FORUM

Annobal Rufus was also responsible for the construction of the city's first market in 9–8BC, which contained two tholoi (kiosks) that served as a space for shops. This was separate from the forum, the main civic area, located near the port. The forum included a major temple to the Roman imperial cult as well as civic buildings such as the *curia* (or council chamber) and a basilica where legal cases could be heard.

THE SEVERAN FORUM

During the 3rd century AD, no doubt under the influence of Septimius Severus, a further forum was developed next to the Wadi Lebdah, this time with generous use of imported marble. The open space was dominated by a temple, which was set on a high podium, and the complex included a grand basilica.

Left: The vast theatre

Above: Gorgon mask

BATHHOUSES

During the reign of the emperor Hadrian in the 2nd century AD, an aqueduct was built to feed the needs of the city. This allowed the construction of a major set of baths in AD126–127 near the Wadi Lebdah. A further set of baths, the Hunting Baths, also dating to the 2nd century AD, were found under sand dunes at the western edge of the city. These were decorated inside with painted scenes of hunting. Both these complexes contained the usual set of cold, warm and hot rooms, and reflect the way the city had adopted the cultural trappings of the Roman Empire.

TRIUMPHAL ARCH

Septimius Severus revisited his home city in AD203 and granted it new status. A triumphal arch was built to commemorate the visit, showing the emperor being greeted by the civic officials.

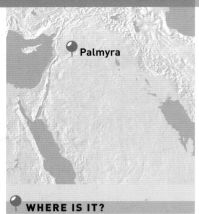

Palmyra

WHERE IS IT?

In eastern Syria, to the northeast of Damascus

GENERAL INFO

For more information on Palmyra visit the following websites: whc.unesco.org/en/list/23; www.syriatourism.org

PALMYRA

A TRADING CITY IN AN OASIS ON THE NORTHERN EDGE OF THE SYRIAN DESERT, WHERE IMPRESSIVE REMAINS RECALL THE RICH HISTORY OF THE PALMYRA EMPIRE DURING THE REIGN OF QUEEN ZENOBIA.

Palmyra (also known as Tadmor) was in effect the border settlement on the caravan route between the Euphrates and the Mediterranean. A Roman garrison was established during the reign of the emperor Tiberius (AD14–37) and the emperor Hadrian granted the city free status in AD129. From 267 to 272 Queen Zenobia, who was captured by Rome, ruled the city.

TEMPLE OF BEL

The Temple of Bel, one of the local gods of Palmyra, was constructed in AD32. It seems to have been inspired by the great temple-building projects in other parts of the Roman province of Syria. This stood in a large colonnaded space that inscriptions suggest was constructed between AD17 and 19. Entered by a monumental triple gate, the sanctuary (or propylon) was on the western side. Approached by a monumental staircase, the entrance to the temple itself was on the long side rather than the normal classical shorter end.

TEMPLE OF BAALSHAMIN

This temple was dedicated AD130–131 by Malé, a member of the local elite of Palmyra who was associated with the visit of Hadrian to the city. This was of a standard classical design with four columns, two deep, across the narrow end. An earlier temple on the site is recorded in AD67.

THE THEATRE

A small theatre seems to have been added to the city in the wake of Hadrian's visit. Access was through a gateway from one of the colonnaded streets. There was a monumental classical stage building. Other classical elements in the city included the creation of a central administrative centre or agora.

Left: The theatre at Palmyra

Right: Roman temple of Baalshamin

THE TRIPYLON

Three roads lead from this unusual tripartite arch. It was the focal point for the colonnaded road entering the city from Damascus, and another of the roads led to the Temple of Bel. These colonnaded streets that are such a feature of cities in the eastern Roman Empire provided space for shops and merchants.

HOUSES

A number of domestic properties have been excavated. These seem to have had a central courtyard. Some have a colonnaded anteroom leading off the court in front of the main reception room. In others there is a standard classical dining room leading directly from the central area.

TOMBS

The tombs were constructed in monumental towers that are found on the periphery of the settlement (such as the Valley of the Tombs). These frequently contain portraits of the individuals in Roman dress, though the texts giving the names of the deceased were cut in a local Aramaic script.

THE WALLS

Traces of the walls may belong to the period of Late Antiquity though some may date to the 3rd century AD when the city was besieged by the Roman emperor Aurelian. The walls seem to have enclosed some 121ha (300 acres). A Roman military unit was apparently garrisoned in the city and is attested by funerary inscriptions. The Roman emperor Diocletian (AD284–305) established a fortress here to guard against the threat of Parthia.

Right: Monumental arch at the archaeological site, with an Arab castle visible in the distance

AFRICA

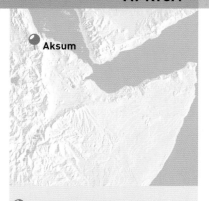

WHERE IS IT?

The city of Aksum lies inland, in the Tigray region of the Ethiopian Highlands

GENERAL INFO

The Ethiopian Ministry of Culture and Tourism website (www. tourismethiopia.org) contains invaluable travel information and suggestions for tours to the country's historical and archaeological attractions

AKSUM

THE CENTRE OF A SOPHISTICATED AFRICAN IRON AGE SOCIETY THAT FLOURISHED IN THE FIRST HALF OF THE FIRST MILLENNIUM AD, THE INFLUENCE OF AKSUM, AND ITS ARCHITECTURE ESPECIALLY, ENDURED FOR MANY CENTURIES.

Pre-Christian architecture from sites near Aksum itself reveals that Aksumite culture originated in the traditions of Semitic-speaking African peoples whose forebears had immigrated from southern Arabia around the middle of the first millennium BC. A disc and crescent motif, the symbol of a South Arabian moon-god, appears on a fifth- to sixth-century BC Aksumite altar and later on coins. The fact that Aksum minted its own coins, of gold, silver and bronze, inscribed in Greek and the indigenous language, Ge'ez, testifies to the importance of trade centred on the Red Sea. Its ruler (the 'negusa negast', or 'King of Kings') headed a confederation of diverse territories, lesser kings, vassals and chiefs. Through its ports, Aksum traded a variety of local products, including ivory, brass and copper and slaves, with the Mediterranean world as well as Arabia, India and beyond. Aksum itself was probably primarily a ceremonial and political centre.

BURIALS

Before conversion to Christianity under the fourth-century AD king Ezana, tombs were marked by stelae,

Right: Detail of the Great Stela in the northern part of the main Stelae Park

Opposite: A tapering stela towers over the site at Aksum

tall, upright stones, some carved. Dated burials have been assigned to the third to fourth centuries AD. Some graves are shafts dug into the rock and joined by corridors, others are elaborate constructions with vaulted ceilings, granite roofs and brickwork. Robbed in antiquity, the Tomb of the Brick Arches contained traces of rich grave goods, including items of gold and ivory.

EXCAVATED BUILDINGS

Excavations since 1906 have exposed three large buildings that were initially interpreted as palaces. They are now thought to have been shared apartment complexes or residential compounds rather than royal quarters. Probably two storeys, they were made of rubble and mud in a timber frame on a raised platform. Their age is uncertain, but they are believed to date to the fourth to fifth centuries BC. The Cathedral of Mary of Zion at Aksum is built on the site of an important earlier church, and was probably constructed in the early 6th century AD.

THE DECLINE

Islamic power spread across northern and eastern Africa from the seventh century AD. Aksum declined in the face of political and economic challenges. With Islamic influence increasing in the region, Christian Aksum may have become isolated, with trade shifting away from the Red Sea towards the Persian Gulf. After Aksum's decline a new centre arose to the south, but the city's heyday was remembered in the continuing use of Aksumite architectural details in religious buildings elsewhere.

Lalibela &
Imraha Kristos

WHERE IS IT?
Northern Ethiopia

GENERAL INFO
The Lalibela churches are visited
by many tourists and pilgrims;
knowledgeable guides can be hired
on site, but are not compulsory

LALIBELA AND
IMRAHA KRISTOS

LALIBELA IS FAMOUS FOR ITS 11 CHURCHES SCULPTED FROM THE PINKISH
ROCK OF THE LASTA MOUNTAINS. AFTER THE DECLINE OF AKSUM A NEW
CHRISTIAN CENTRE, INITIALLY KNOWN AS ROHA, ROSE HERE, RULED FROM
AD1137 BY KINGS OF THE ZAGWE DYNASTY.

According to legend, the Zagwe King Lalibela (*r*AD1189–1229) was poisoned by a rival. While unconscious he saw a vision of rock-cut churches, which he then vowed to build. Though attributed to him, the churches were probably built over several centuries. The churches of Merkurios and Gabriel-Raphael may have originally been part of older structures, perhaps a palace and a fortified complex dating to around the seventh century AD.

KING LALIBELA'S LEGACY

Lalibela's assumption of power coincided with the Muslim occupation of Jerusalem by Salah-ad-Din (Saladin). The settlement that would later bear Lalibela's name was deliberately modelled as a 'New Jerusalem'. A canalized stream is named after the River Jordan, one church is named after Jerusalem's Church of Golgotha and another structure dating to Lalibela's reign is known as the Tomb of Adam.

ETHIOPIAN ROCK-CHURCH ARCHITECTURE

The churches have been cut from the rock so that some are entirely freestanding, or monolithic, whereas others remain partially attached to the mountainside and some are surrounded by trenches. Underground tunnels and chambers connect different structures. Ethiopia was a centre for early Christians from far and wide and displays diverse architectural influences, from indigenous Aksumite to Byzantine.

Details in several of the churches continue the long tradition of Aksumite architecture and celebrate the heyday of that city. The monolithic church of Beta Medhane Alem partly replicates the design of the Cathedral of Mary of Zion at Aksum (around the sixth century AD). At over 30m (98ft) in length it is the largest

Left: St. George's Church, Lalibela

Right: Church of Beta Medhane Alem (Saviour of the World)

of the churches at Lalibela, with a striking exterior colonnade of square pillars. It houses the Afro Ayigeba, a decorated cross, 60cm (24in) long, believed to have healing powers. It is now constantly guarded after being stolen in 1997 and sold on the illegal antiquities market.

ST. GEORGE'S CHURCH

Set slightly apart, the 13th-century Beta Giyorgis, or House of St. George, is dedicated to Ethiopia's patron saint. Perhaps the best-preserved and most architecturally interesting church, it has a cruciform floor plan and a ceiling carved with bas-relief crosses.

IMRAHA KRISTOS CHURCH

Twenty kilometres (12 miles) northeast of Lalibela is another notable 11th–12th century rock-hewn church, located inside a large cave. Imraha Kristos, named after another ruler of the Zagwe dynasty, is a remarkable example of Aksumite architecture, with an elaborate ceiling and extraordinary paintings of mythical creatures. Like the Lalibela churches, it is still in use today.

Right: Imraha Kristos monastery, northeast Lalibela

Below: Interior of Christian church of Beta Medhane Alem

Saharan
Rock Art

WHERE IS IT?

Southwestern Libya, near the
Algerian border

GENERAL INFO

The sites are part of a proposed
'archaeological park' and visitors
require a guide. Numerous
operators offer tours, many
including the nearby ancient city
of Ghat

SAHARAN ROCK ART

THE FEZZAN, OR SOUTHWESTERN LIBYAN SAHARA, IS RICH IN ROCK ART.
ROCK CARVINGS, OR PETROGLYPHS, ABOUND IN THE MESSAK SETTAFET,
THE 'BLACK PLATEAU', AND THE MESSAK MELLET OR 'WHITE PLATEAU'. ROCK
PAINTINGS SURVIVE IN THE ADJACENT TADRART ACACUS MOUNTAINS.

Rock art in these areas dates to times when the
Sahara was a well-watered landscape that supported a
varied wildlife and, about 7,000 years ago, herders with
cattle. Most scholars believe that the earliest rock art
was made by hunter-gatherers about 10,000 years ago,
others that they post-date the introduction of domestic
animals. Paintings rarely contain enough carbon for
radiocarbon dating and petroglyphs cannot be dated by
that technique. Researchers have mainly deduced age
sequences based on styles and subjects. Excavations
at the cave of Uan Muhuggiag uncovered painted rock
fragments stratified in deposits dated to about 5,000
years ago.

BIG GAME ART

In the numerous sites of the Wadi Teshuinat valley
(Tadrart Acacus), the various styles of Saharan rock
art can be seen in one area. The Bubalus or 'Big
Game' phase includes both petroglyphs and rock
paintings. The subjects are large animals including
giraffe, antelope and elephant, in a naturalistic style.
Images of an African buffalo, *Homoiceras antiquus*, that
became extinct about 5,000 years ago, are a clue to the
antiquity of these images.

HUMANS AND CATTLE IN ART

The Roundhead phase is characterized by paintings
of human figures with faceless round heads. The
activities portrayed include dances and hunting scenes.
They are interpreted as initiation ceremonies and other
rituals, with some themes possibly deriving from
long-lost mythologies.

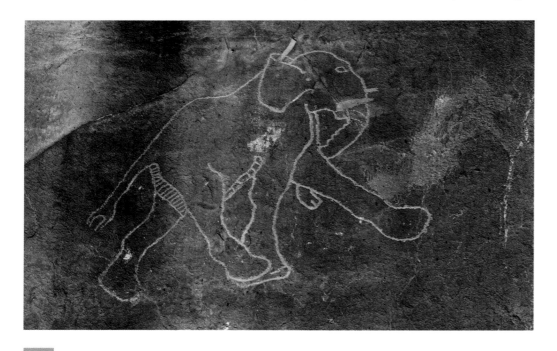

**Right: Rock engravings, Messak Mellet, southwest desert
in Libya**

Left: Detail of 'Big Game' rock painting

Cattle are abundant in both paintings and petroglyphs after c7,000 years ago, indicating the importance of the new herding way of life. Images of the Pastoral or Bovidian phase include figures of cows being milked and other everyday activities. This does not preclude symbolic meanings, since archaeological evidence suggests that cattle were sometimes important in religious rites. Many paintings of the Pastoral phase are technically skilled and finely detailed.

LATER DEPICTIONS

Images, of chariots and of stylized humans with bodies composed of triangular forms probably date to after 1000BC. The Garamantes, mentioned by the historian Herodotus in the fifth century BC, belonged to a sophisticated early Libyan state. Horses, chariots and camels were introduced to the area during the time of the Garamantian state and date these images to the most recent phase of the rock art.

THE FIGHTING CATS

The Wadi Matkhandush in the Messak Settafet is an area rich in petroglyphs. Images include giraffe, crocodile, rhinoceros and circular abstract designs. Especially famous is a carved boulder with images known as the 'fighting cats'. It depicts two feline-like creatures standing on their hind legs, with four small birds between them and a third 'cat' to one side. The bodies of the figures were then polished smooth.

SOUTHERN AFRICAN ROCK ART

SOUTHERN AFRICAN ROCK ART MADE BY INDIGENOUS SAN (BUSHMAN) HUNTER-GATHERERS IS VISIBLE IN THOUSANDS OF SITES IN SHALLOW CAVES AND ON ROCK OUTCROPS.

Southern African Rock Art

WHERE IS IT?

The Drakensberg Mountains lie north of Pietermaritzburg, in KwaZulu-Natal, South Africa; Twyfelfontein is 90km (56 miles) west of the tiny Namibian town of Khorixas in Damaraland, northwestern Namibia; 150km (93 miles) to the south is the Brandberg, famous for its rock paintings

GENERAL INFO

Drakensberg rock painting sites open to the public are in reserves managed by Ezemvelo KZN Wildlife

The oldest indirectly radiocarbon-dated paintings on cave walls are at least 3,600 years old. In the Drakensberg, the painting tradition continued into the 19th century AD. Petroglyphs (rock carvings), found especially on the arid interior plateau, are largely of unknown age. Once thought to be literal depictions of everyday life, rock art is now known to have deeper religious meanings. The artists principally drew people and animals, rarely landscape features. Abstract designs are rare in paintings but more common in petroglyphs. Some sites, such as Giant's Castle Main Caves (Drakensberg), contain hundreds of images in diverse styles, the paintings accumulating over many centuries. The abundant rock art of nearby Didima (Ndedema) Gorge is known worldwide.

GAME PASS

At Kamberg in the central Drakensberg, Game Pass is a shallow shelter with well-preserved polychrome paintings of remarkable skill. The intriguing imagery includes a composition of men in *karosses* (skin cloaks) amid a herd of delicately shaded eland—the largest antelope and the San creator's favourite creature. A famous composition depicts a staggering eland and figures with both human and animal features (therianthropes). One, with hooves, ears and its body apparently covered in hair, grasps the eland's tail.

The therianthropes are open to different interpretations. Some researchers regard them as San 'shamans'. This reading draws on knowledge of modern San who cure sickness using ritual trance and may experience hallucinatory visions. The figure holding the stumbling eland's tail is therefore said to

herbivorous animal. Eland and hippo-like creatures appear as 'rain animals' in compositions once seen as simple hunting scenes, but now known to depict rainmaking.

TWYFELFONTEIN

Named after a spring in Namibia's otherwise parched landscape, Twyfelfontein is an area rich in petroglyphs. A dozen sites contain over 5,000 individual images on sandstone. They were made either by 'pecking' designs with a hammerstone or by incising fine lines with a stone burin. Unusually, overhangs with rock paintings are also found here, though paintings and petroglyphs generally occur in different areas. Excavations have uncovered later Stone Age artefacts from between 2,000 and 6,000 years ago.

depict prehistoric trance experiences and 'shamanic' control of supernaturally potent animals.

Alternatively, therianthropes may represent the spirits of dead kin whom the living called upon for success in hunting and in controlling the rain. Nineteenth-century San saw the rain as a large

Above: Bushman art showing men and eland at Game Pass, Kamberg

Right: Twyfelfontein engraving, Namibia

DEPICTIONS IN ROCK ART

The giraffe is the most frequently depicted animal, but subjects include elephant, rhino, zebra and ostrich, human footprints and animal tracks. Non-figurative imagery includes various geometric motifs. Cupules—small hollows made by pecking or grinding—are an enigmatic feature in some sites.

Right: San rock art found in Twyfelfontein, Namibia

STERKFONTEIN CAVE

STERKFONTEIN IS AN IMPORTANT SOUTHERN AFRICAN FOSSIL SITE THAT HAS YIELDED SPECIES OF EARLY HUMAN AS WELL AS ABUNDANT FOSSIL ANIMAL BONES.

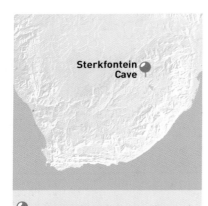

Sterkfontein
Cave

WHERE IS IT?
Gauteng Province, South Africa, in the Isaac Stegmann Nature Reserve about 10km (6 miles) north of Krugersdorp

WHEN TO VISIT
Open daily, the site has a small museum

GENERAL INFO
Bookings can be made for guided tours throughout the day (9–4)

Sterkfontein is one of several fossil-bearing sites in northeastern South Africa that have led to the area being known as 'The Cradle of Humankind'. The fossils and stone artefacts recovered have provided rich insights into human evolution and behaviour.

EARLY HUMAN REMAINS

In the 1930s, mining of limestone at Sterkfontein alerted the palaeoanthropologist Robert Broom to the presence of human and animal fossils. The bones accumulated after being washed (or falling) into shafts, known as avens, leading to underground caverns. The bones fossilized and the deposits became cemented into a solid matrix known as breccia. The Sterkfontein deposits are divided into six geological layers or 'members'.

AFRICAN SOUTHERN APE

Among the fossils drilled from the breccia were fragments of a small hominid known as *Australopithecus africanus* ('African southern ape'). Regarded by most palaeoanthropologists as a hominid species ancestral to the genus *Homo*, the slightly-built, small-brained *A. africanus* walked upright but retained ape-like anatomical features including fingers adapted for climbing and a tree-dwelling existence.

The first australopithecine known was a child's skull uncovered by limestone mining at Taung in 1925. At Sterkfontein, Broom discovered the first known fossils of an adult *australopithecine* in 1936, and in 1947 a remarkably well-preserved skull, dated to between 2.8 and 2.6 million years ago. Initially classified as *Plesianthropus transvaalensis*, it became world famous as 'Mrs Ples'. Subsequent researchers have identified it as *Australopithecus africanus*. It may in fact be male. The most exciting find of recent years is a well-preserved *A. africanus* specimen from Member 2. It has been dubbed 'Little Foot' and although the specimen is still being worked on it is thought to be at least 3.3 million years old (see box).

In 1994 the palaeoanthropologist Ron Clarke found four hominid foot bones excavated many years ago and stored. He recognized them as belonging to a creature that walked upright. Astonishingly, a team found the spot from where the bones were originally drilled within two days and matched them to the rest of the individual, still in situ. It is still being excavated but seems to be an almost complete skeleton—a rare find.

ARTEFACTS AND DATES

No stone tools were found in the older members that contain *A. africanus* remains, but several thousand stone artefacts have been excavated from Member 5, dated to between 2 and 1.5 million years ago. They include Oldowan artefacts, the oldest known stone tool industry, and Acheulean artefacts, belonging to a worldwide artefact tradition, or 'industry', that emerged in East Africa around 1.6 million years ago.

Ongoing research focuses on excavation and comparison and classification of the hominid remains. Dating the deposits is a key problem because the sediments are not volcanic, and standard techniques such as potassium-argon dating cannot be used.

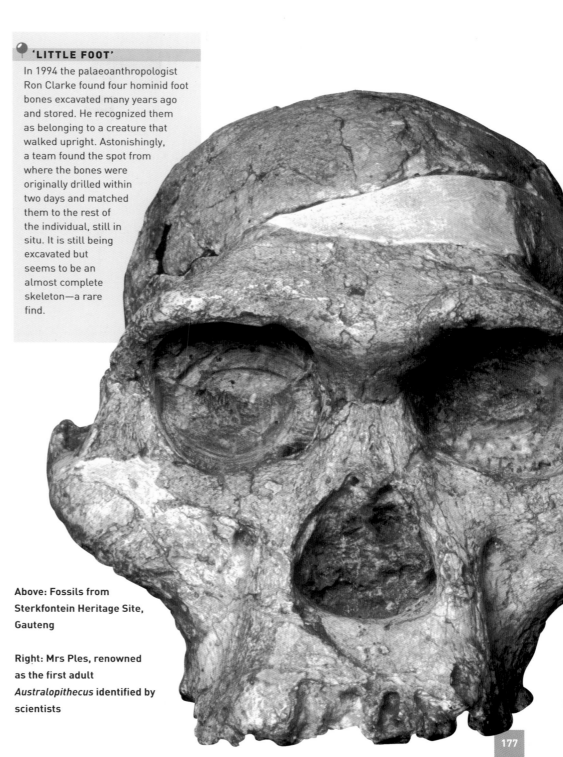

Above: Fossils from Sterkfontein Heritage Site, Gauteng

Right: Mrs Ples, renowned as the first adult *Australopithecus* identified by scientists

Meroe

MEROE

IN NUBIA, SOUTH OF EGYPT, THE KINGDOM OF KUSH FLOURISHED ALONG THE MIDDLE NILE FROM ABOUT 2500BC TILL THE EARLY 1ST MILLENNIUM AD. MEROE WAS ITS LAST GREAT CENTRE.

WHERE IS IT?
320km (199 miles) northeast of present-day Khartoum, near Kabushia, Sudan

GENERAL INFO
A newly constructed tarred highway runs from Khartoum to Atbara, 100km (62 miles) south of Meroe. For tourists travelling by train, this town is also a major railway junction. From here, hire a car or find a local tour operator

and sorghum, with iron production an important industry. The Meroitic language eventually replaced Egyptian, and Meroitic script, still undeciphered today, appeared on public architecture.

MEROE DISCOVERIES

Excavations at Meroe have revealed a once prosperous town with palaces, baths and residences as well as locations with evidence of manufacturing by skilled artisans. One 'palace' is attached to a temple of the Egyptian god Amun. In contrast, the Meroitic towns of Musawwarat el Sufra and Naqa, 20km (12 miles) to the south, have temples to Apedemak, the lion-headed Nubian hunter-warrior god.

After 270BC Meroe was the exclusive burial place of Kushite royalty. The later Kushite kings were buried in subterranean tombs topped by pyramids in a distinctive Kushitic style. Though many are now ruined, over 200 pyramids are found in three cemeteries (see box).

DECLINE OF MEROE

Alexander the Great attempted unsuccessfully to invade Meroe in 322BC but withdrew when facing a Meroitic army. In the early current era, Meroe clashed with the Romans, who were then in command of Egypt. The Romans invaded in 24BC in retaliation for Nubian incursions into Egypt. A bronze head of the emperor Augustus, found buried at Meroe and now housed in the British Museum, dates to this time period.

The end of Meroe is often attributed to an invasion by the Christian king of Aksum in about AD330 but probably declined because of wider economic and political pressures. Both Aksum, to the southeast, and Meroe exported the same goods, but Aksum, closer to the Red Sea, enjoyed a strategic advantage. Clashes with surrounding nomadic herders, the Blemmyes, may have contributed to the city's decline.

Above: Detail of stonework on a Kushite pyramid

Left and next page: The pyramids of Meroe

🔎 KUSHITE BURIAL PYRAMIDS

Kushitic pyramids emphasized height rather than mass and volume and are steeper-sided than their Egyptian counterparts. Tombs were cut into the rock beneath, with the pyramids as grave markers, not as burial chambers. The subterranean structures became more elaborate over time. The pyramids, made first of stone, later brick, were laid in stepped courses that were then lime-plastered. Traces of exotic grave goods testify to Meroe's wealth and the reach of its influence.

Over the millennia, power relations between Kush and Egypt shifted to and fro. Five Kushite kings had ruled Egypt as pharaohs of the 25th Dynasty (c730–661BC) before the balance of power reverted again. Egypt occupied areas of Nubia in 571BC and Meroe, to the south, rose as the new Kushite capital.

TRADING ROUTES

For centuries Nubia and the surrounding desert supplied Egypt with trade goods from the deserts nearby. Ivory, pelts, iron, semi-precious stones, exotic animals and slaves were among the commodities sent north by caravan in exchange for luxury items such as glass, textiles, wines and oils. The Meroitic economy was based on cattle herding and cultivation of millet

OLDUVAI GORGE

OLDUVAI GORGE IS A 90M (295FT) DEEP RAVINE WITH ABOUT
48KM (30 MILES) OF GEOLOGICAL DEPOSITS EXPOSED BY WATER
EROSION. THE LAYERS OF VOLCANIC ASH AND LAVA HAVE
PRESERVED THE FOSSIL REMAINS OF HOMINIDS AND EARLY
HUMANS, AS WELL AS MANY ANIMAL SPECIES, SOME DATING
BACK OVER TWO MILLION YEARS.

⦿ WHERE IS IT?

In Northern Tanzania, in the
Ngorongoro conservation area
and on the road to the Serengeti
National Park

⦿ GENERAL INFO

Archaeological finds are on view
in a site museum and walking
tours into the gorge can be
arranged throughout the year. It is
compulsory to be accompanied by
a guide

Olduvai became world-famous through the work of
Louis and Mary Leakey who pioneered archaeological
and palaeontological work here in the 1950s. Olduvai's
fossil evidence was important in establishing that our
species evolved in Africa.

HUMAN FOSSILS

Remains of more than 60 individuals have been
recovered from seven layers of deposit, known as
'beds', that range from about 10m (33ft) to over
50m (164ft) in depth. The oldest, Bed I, contained
1.75 million-year-old fossils of a species first called
Zinjanthropus and dubbed 'Nutcracker man' because of
its large jaw, adapted for a fibrous vegetable diet. It is
now reclassified as *Paranthropus boisei* (or by some as
Australopithecus boisei). This heavily-built species is not
thought to be in the direct line of human ancestry.

   Also in Bed I were fossils of a possible human
ancestor species, *Homo habilis*, a species with
anatomical features intermediate between
Australopithecus and *Homo*. The anatomy of its hand
bones suggested it had the dexterity to make and use
artefacts, hence the name *habilis* ('handy man'). Fossils
of *Homo ergaster*, a name given to African specimens of
the large-brained human species *Homo erectus*, have
been excavated from Bed II. The youngest formations,

STONE AGE LIVING SITES

The remarkable finds at Olduvai include areas that may represent ancient campsites, located in old stream channels. Sites where stone tools and animal remains have been found in close proximity have been interpreted as butchery sites. A rough circle of stones excavated by Mary Leakey at site DK, in the oldest level at Olduvai (Bed I), may have been a foundation for a very early structure, though it cannot be conclusively established that it was man-made. Like the classification of fossil hominid materials, these interpretations are subject to debate and ongoing research.

the Ndutu and Naisiusiu Beds, were deposited after 400,000 years ago and contain artefacts dated to the Middle and Later Stone Age.

USE OF TOOLS

The sequence of layers at Olduvai contains the world's longest continuous record of successive stone tool industries. However, hominids and stone artefacts have never been found in direct association. Early stone artefacts dating to 2.6 million years ago, consisting of modified pebbles used as chopping and scraping tools, were first described at Olduvai, in levels that also yielded *Homo habilis* fossils. The Oldowan artefacts are succeeded in Bed II by more sophisticated tools belonging to the Acheulean industry. Acheulean tools include the classic handaxes that appear throughout the world in the early Stone Age.

Left: Olduvai Gorge, Ngorongoro National Park, Tanzania

Below: Acheulean hand axe

GREAT ZIMBABWE

ITS NAME DERIVING FROM THE SHONA WORD DZIMBABWE,
MEANING STONE HOUSE OR VENERATED HOUSE, GREAT
ZIMBABWE IS ONE OF SOUTHERN AFRICA'S PREMIER
ARCHAEOLOGICAL SITES.

Great
Zimbabwe

● WHERE IS IT?
Located 28km (17 miles) southeast
of the town of Masvingo in south-
central Zimbabwe

● GENERAL INFO
Information on visiting the area
can be found on the Zimbabwe
Tourism Authority's website (www.
zimbabwetourism.co.zw). It is fairly
easy to navigate these ruins. There
are two paths going up; the ancient
path, which is more difficult, and
the modern purpose-built path,
making for an easier ascent

**Right: The ruins of Great Zimbabwe are
spread over a large area**

The centre of a flourishing Shona state, the settlement
dates to the archaeological time period known as
the Later Iron Age, which began cAD1000. Later
Iron Age economies were based on iron production,
cattle keeping and the cultivation of various cereal
crops. Great Zimbabwe is the largest of a number
of *dzimbabwes* that derived their wealth from Indian
Ocean trade. Gold, copper and ivory were exported via
the port of Sofala in Mozambique and traded north
where Swahili intercontinental trading posts flourished
along the coast of present-day Kenya and Tanzania.
Great Zimbabwe was visited by Swahili traders and
sought by the Portuguese, who thought it was the
biblical city of Ophir, or a city linked to the queen of
Sheba. Exotic goods, including oriental ceramics,
trade beads and Near Eastern glassware found during
excavations, indicate trade contact with places as
distant as India, China and Persia.

EARLY ORIGINS

Speculation once attributed the building of Great
Zimbabwe to exotic foreigners, but excavations have
long since shown that the techniques of building in
stone and way of life were those of local indigenous
peoples. The site extends over almost 728ha (1,800
acres), with the Great Enclosure and Hill Ruin identified
as royal residences, the design, layout and walling
distinguishing the elite areas. Unwalled homesteads
were scattered throughout the surrounding area.

The population of the town and surrounds may have exceeded 10,000. The Later Iron Age marks the beginning of socially stratified societies in southern Africa. Various features of Great Zimbabwe are thought to symbolize royal power. Architecture, sculpture and the organization of space served to underline the distinction between royalty and ordinary people and to emphasize the special relationship of the elite to the land.

THE GREAT ENCLOSURE

The Great Enclosure is defined by a curving drystone granite wall, 5m (16ft) thick and up to 20m (66ft) high, topped in places by bands of decorative stonework in a chevron design. Thatched structures were built within. A famous feature is the Conical Tower, a symbolic structure of unknown significance. Moulded clay served as furniture, with raised areas as seats and sleeping platforms.

A SETTLEMENT IN DECLINE

The decline of Great Zimbabwe by the 16th century may relate to environmental depletion, with over-harvesting of the wood needed to fuel smelting furnaces. A decline in the gold trade may have been another factor, and internal political strife cannot be discounted. Other *dzimbabwes* to the north and south became key centres in subsequent years.

Left: An example of the curving drystone walling at Great Zimbabwe

Right: Carved soapstone (steatite) bird of the type crafted in the 13th–15th centuries in Great Zimbabwe

THE ZIMBABWE BIRDS
Large soapstone sculptures of birds found during early investigations probably came from the base of the Hill Ruin. The birds do not represent any actual species but are imaginative and symbolic, perhaps referring to the ancestors. They display some human features, such as feet with five claws. The birds perch on top of tall columns that may have been placed in prominent positions as icons of royal authority.

ASIA

Left: The carved faces of future Buddhas adorn
the towers of the Bayon, Angkor

Angkor

WHERE IS IT?

Near Siem Reap, Cambodia

GENERAL INFO

The huge complex of Angkor has become one of the foremost tourist attractions in Asia, and several temples and other structures are still being restored and should be open to visits within the next year or two

ANGKOR

THE IMMENSE COMPLEX OF TEMPLES AND OTHER BUILDINGS THAT FORMED THE CITY THAT IS NOW CALLED ANGKOR, IN MODERN CAMBODIA, WAS ONE OF THE GREAT WONDERS OF ANCIENT ASIA.

Angkor was the capital of southeast Asia's Khmer empire, from the first century BC to the 15th century AD, when it was pillaged by neighbouring Siam. Today, after years of neglect and damage caused by warfare, it has become one of the most impressive and popular tourist destinations of the world. Although the word

'Angkor' comes from a Sanskrit term for 'holy city', Angkor itself was not a city, but a huge, sprawling complex of temples, monuments, reservoirs and canals that developed in different stages over the centuries. It is not really known to what extent ordinary people actually lived inside the complex.

Left: Aerial view of Angkor Wat

Right: One of the carved faces of the Bayon

Next spread: Approaching the main entrance of Angkor Wat

ANGKOR THOM COMPLEX

The Khmer kingdom reached its greatest extent under Jayavarman VII, who built the huge complex of Angkor Thom in the 12th century. This complex covers 9sq km (3.5sq miles), and is enclosed by a wall 3km (2 miles) square. Each side is pierced by a great gateway, 23m (75ft) high, which features a tower carved with four faces pointing to the four cardinal directions. Each of these gates is approached by an impressive avenue of carved gods on one side, and demons on the other, carrying a giant serpent across the moat.

ANGKOR WAT COMPLEX

The most famous temple complex of all, Angkor Wat, was built in the 12th century. This great temple blended Hindu cosmology and architecture with pre-existing Khmer beliefs. The enclosure symbolizes the Hindu cosmos, while the temple itself stood for the five peaks of Mount Meru, the abode of the gods.

The Temple of Bapuon is currently being restored. This 'Golden Mountain', built c1060 on three storeys in the centre of Angkor Thom, next to the Bayon, was the spiritual centre until Angkor Wat was built.

ANGKOR'S DECLINE AND REDISCOVERY

It seems likely that a fall in agricultural production may have been a factor in the downfall of Angkorian civilization, along with the military expansion of the Siamese. Rediscovered by a French missionary in 1850, Angkor was studied quite intensively in later decades, and the French colonialists eventually established major programmes to research the archaeology of what was then called Indochina. In the early 1970s, the Angkor region was captured by the Khmer Rouge, who carried out a 20-year period of neglect and destruction, with sculptures being destroyed or illegally sold, and vegetation allowed to encroach on the buildings.

Left: Detail of the Bayon frieze showing cock-fighting

Right: Part of the overgrown Temple of Ta Prohm

MING TOMBS

IN THE YEAR AD1409 EMPEROR YONGLE COMMISSIONED TWO HUGE CONSTRUCTION PROJECTS: THE FORBIDDEN CITY AND HIS OWN MAUSOLEUM, THE FIRST OF ALTOGETHER 13 IMPERIAL TOMBS, BUILT WITHIN 230 YEARS IN THE VALLEY OF CHANGPING.

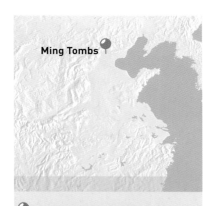

Ming Tombs

WHERE IS IT?

Changping District, northeast of Beijing City (China)

WHEN TO VISIT

Any time of the year. Changling Tomb 8.30 to 5.30; Dingling Tomb 8.30 to 6

GENERAL INFO

Recommended time for a visit is two hours. The Ming tomb valley is well worth seeing. Allow time to enjoy the imperial architecture and the surrounding mountains and vegetation

Thirteen out of the 16 Ming emperors as well as 23 empresses, one highest-ranking concubine and 12 sacrificed imperial concubines were buried in this peaceful valley. The site of the Ming Dynasty Imperial Tombs was carefully chosen according to fen shui (geomancy) principles. The whole process from site selection to building of the tombs as a copy of the imperial palace paid attention to the harmony between the tomb architecture and the surrounding landscape.

ON THE WAY TO THE IMPERIAL TOMBS

A large three-arched gateway, the Grand Red Gate, and the so-called 'Spirit Path', a 7km (4-mile) long road bordered by stone animals and guardian officials, lead to the different tombs. The path is slightly curved to fool evil spirits. The statuary includes pairs of camels, lions, elephants and mythical beasts, such as the *qilin*, a creature of immense virtue referred to as the Chinese unicorn, even though it has two horns. Though varying in architectural complexity, size and furnishings, the tombs are similar in their basic layout: a stone bridge, followed by a front gate, a stela pavilion and a Sacrificial Hall, the Gate of Eminent Favour, the Hall of Eminent Favour, a watchtower and finally the Precious Hall. Visitors are free to stroll around the complex site.

Right: Changling, Ming tomb

THE FATE OF EXCAVATION—CHANGLING TOMB

At present, three tombs are partly open to the public: Changling, the largest; Dingling, whose underground palace has been fully excavated; and Zhaoling. Changling, the tomb of Emperor Yongle's (r1403–1424), is the best preserved of the 13 tombs. Its architecture recalls the Forbidden City—for example, the Hall of Mercy, which comprises an area of 2,000sq m (21,528sq ft). Noteworthy are the 60 gigantic sandalwood columns. The four innermost columns measure 14.3m (47ft) in height. These large trees came from Sichuan and Jiangxi provinces; their transportation over several thousand miles took between two and three years.

DINGLING TOMB

Dingling (the Tomb of Stability) belonged to Emperor Wanli (r1572–1620), his wife, and his favourite concubine. The underground palace was built as a vast marble vault, buried 27m (89ft) underground and divided into five large chambers. It was under archaeological excavation in 1956 and is the only imperial tomb to have been fully excavated since the founding of the People's Republic of China, a situation that is a direct result of the fate which the tomb and its grave goods suffered after the dig. The excavation first revealed an intact tomb, with thousands of items of silk, textiles, wood and porcelain. At this time neither the technology nor the resources were available to store the excavated objects, which led to a deterioration of most of the artefacts.

ZHAOLING TOMB

In 1990 the third mausoleum was opened to the public: Zhaoling, the last resting place for the 12th Ming emperor, Longqing (r1567–1572). After the long period of his father's disastrous regime, he reformed the government and promoted trade with empires in Europe, Africa and other Asian countries. It is the first tomb that has been fully restored to its original plan.

MING TOMBS MUSEUM

The Ming tombs were listed as a UNESCO World Heritage Site in August 2003, along with the imperial tombs of the Qing-Dynasty (1644–1911). The Shisan Ling Bowuguan (Ming Tombs Museum) displays biographies of all the entombed emperors, several burial goods and a detailed wooden reproduction of the Ling'en Dian (Hall of Eminent Favour) and a photo of Mao reclining and reading a newspaper on a half-buried marble incense burner at Changling in 1954.

Left: Watchtower at Changling

Below: Ming Tombs Museum

THE GREAT WALL

THE GREAT WALL IS THE BIGGEST FORTIFICATION CONSTRUCTION IN THE WORLD. IT TWISTS AND TURNS ACROSS THE NORTHERN REACHES OF CHINA LIKE A DRAGON STARTING IN THE EAST AT HUSHAN (THE SO-CALLED 'TIGER MOUNTAIN'), 20KM (12 MILES) FROM DANDONG CITY, IN LIAONING PROVINCE, AND ENDING AT JIAYUGUAN IN GANSU PROVINCE IN THE WEST.

The Great Wall

WHERE IS IT?
Northern reaches of China/ northern borders of China

WHEN TO VISIT
Any time of the year, depending on the different sections

GENERAL INFO
For a panoramic tour of the Great Wall see www.world-heritage-tour. org/asia/china/great-wall/map. html; for detailed history see www. greatwall-of-china.com/

The earliest parts of the Great Wall date back to the 7th century BC, when China was still under the control of numerous feudal states, each of them eager to protect its own frontiers and territory. In this turbulent period the mighty state of the Qin, after long and violent campaigns, defeated the smaller states and unified China in 221BC; a long period of division by feudal lords ended. The Qin territory enlarged greatly, extending to the east, west, south and north. To solve the problem of the intrusion of the northern nomadic Xiongnu tribes, the First August Emperor of the Qin, Qin Shihuangdi (r221–210BC), forced two million slaves, confiscated labourers, captives of war and prisoners to build the 10,000 li (i.e. 5,000km/3,100 miles) Great Wall, a project that lasted 10 years.

BUILDING THE WALL

The building of the wall depended mainly on local resources. It was such a big project that it seemed impossible to build it with identical forms and materials in the different areas. In the early periods the construction was mainly done with the method of so-called 'stamped earth'. Wooden planks were laid parallel to one another as wide apart as the wall's thickness. Clay, mixed with water, was filled in and people packed it down with their feet and square iron pestles. In some parts the craggy landscape did not allow continuous building of the wall, and natural barriers such as mountain ridges were used to link the different parts of the wall. In order to protect the Chinese Empire from Mongolian invaders, the wall was periodically rebuilt and modified throughout history by each of the following reigning dynasties.

Left: Snow-covered mountains beyond the roofs of Jiayuguan

THE GREAT WALL OF THE MING DYNASTY

The main parts of the Great Wall we see today were built in the Ming Dynasty (AD1364–1644). As the war tactics and the weapons of enemies changed, the wall was not only used as a permanent fortification for defence but also to be prepared for any battle along this defence line. The Chinese rulers connected the regional wall parts and reconstructed the old weather-beaten parts to build a wide and high wall; they also added watch- and beacon towers. The complex structure demanded a new material: bricks. Recent discoveries of kilns for bricks along the wall in northern Hebei province, excavated just 500m (1,640ft) from the Great Wall itself and buried under two separate cornfields, showed the efficiency employed in building it—5,000 grey bricks could be baked in one kiln, the perfect material for a strong fortification.

MILITARY CONTROL

To strengthen the military control of the northern frontiers, the Ming authorities divided the Great Wall into nine zones and placed each under the control of a Zhen (garrison headquarters). With an average height of 10m (33ft) and a width of 5m (16ft), the wall now ran up and down along the mountain ridges and valleys from east to west. Passes were included to allow controlled entry to, and exit from, the home territory. They were situated at key positions, usually on trade routes. Beacon towers, providing accommodation for soldiers as well as storage of diverse materials or even livestock, were used as signal towers on hilltops. Communication between the army units along the length of the Great Wall was very important. During daylight hours smoke signals were used, while at night lanterns and beacon fires were employed. Other means of signalling included the use of flags, clappers, drums and bells.

Left: Walkers on the Great Wall

LEGEND HAS IT

The Chinese have a saying: "If you haven't climbed the Great Wall you're not a real man". For a long time people believed that the Great Wall was the only man-made building that could be seen with the unaided eye from space or from the moon. This has been proved to be a myth.

THE TERRACOTTA ARMY

A HUGE ARMY OF MORE THAN 2,000 TERRACOTTA SOLDIERS GUARDS THE TOMB OF THE FIRST AUGUST EMPEROR OF THE QIN DYNASTY (221–206BC), QIN SHI HUANGDI. IT IS THE MUTE WITNESS OF THE POWER OF THE EMPEROR AND THE SPECIALIZED SKILLS OF THE CRAFTSMEN AND FORCED LABOURERS WHO WORKED ON THE PROJECT.

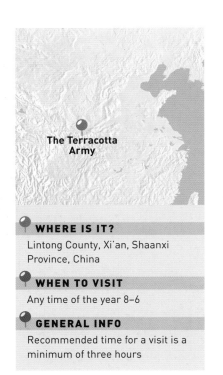

The Terracotta Army

WHERE IS IT?

Lintong County, Xi'an, Shaanxi Province, China

WHEN TO VISIT

Any time of the year 8–6

GENERAL INFO

Recommended time for a visit is a minimum of three hours

After the long period of the so-called Warring States (5th–3rd century BC), the First Emperor, Qin Shi Huangdi (r221–210BC), unified China. He standardized weights, the writing system, administration and currency. His large tomb with the Terracotta Army is testimony to his military power and his concern for the palace in the underworld.

FORTUNATE COINCIDENCE

In 1974 farmers were digging a well in a field in Lintong, about 35km (22 miles) east of Xi'an. But instead of striking water they found clay legs, arms and heads, which led to the first pit of Qin Shi Huangdi's necropolis. It contained over 200 life-size clay soldiers in battle formation, which originally were heavily armed. Infantry soldiers and cavalry with big horses were lined up in the pits. Since then 180 more pits have been excavated, but the 8,099 clay soldiers, acrobats, fishermen, animals and other figures have still not been entirely restored. Since 1987 the site has been on the UNESCO World Heritage list.

Left and above: Soldiers in the side pits

MEGALOMANIA OR WORLD WONDER

As soon as the First Emperor ascended the throne, work began on his necropolis at Mount Li. Seven hundred thousand slaves and craftsmen were forced to dig out the pits for the living areas. He would plan his tomb as an underground palace with living quarters, stables, kitchens, parks, ceremonial palaces and landscaping. It was thus a miniature copy of his imperial household. The complex had not been finished when the emperor died in 210BC, but the tomb itself was ready for the burial. According to the *Records of the Historian* from the court writer Sima Qian (145–86BC), the tomb chamber was furnished with thousands of precious grave goods and built with mountains made from rocks, streams reproduced with mercury, and a depiction of the celestial constellations, representing a colourful microcosm of the universe. The tomb itself

has not been excavated so far. It may have been looted as were the quarters of the guarding soldiers soon after the completion of the necropolis, and plundered by the troops of the emperor of the later Han Dynasty. Burning, destruction of the tomb pits and plundering of the precious weapons ruined the whole structure.

Nevertheless, in July 2007 archaeologists used remote sensing to examine the tomb. They found a 30m (98ft) tall building above the tomb, with four stepped walls, each having nine steps. While testing the soil they detected high levels of mercury around the tomb. Will Sima Qian's *Records* turn out to be true?

NEW DISCOVERIES

Above ground, the rectangular layout of the necropolis resembled that of a palace, with an inner and outer wall made of pounded earth, no longer intact. Side halls, foundations of retiring halls, ancestor temples and provision offices were found and identified by inscriptions on ceramic shards. Pits with bronze chariots and horses, livestock like cattle and also exotic animals such as tigers and pandas lay within the inner reaches of the necropolis. Recently a new pit has been discovered. It lies 900m (2,953ft) outside the northeastern corner of the outer wall. Bronze cranes, swans, ducks and other water birds are placed along an artificial stream, accompanied by terracotta musicians.

'AS IF THEY WERE ALIVE'

The most spectacular burial outside the tomb proper is the Terracotta Army. The logistical problems in procuring material such as clay, pigments, firewood and lacquer must have been considerable. Moreover, the organization of the labour force must have been no less demanding. Four pits were reserved for the powerful army. High-ranking officers, soldiers, crossbow archers and horses were all handmade by mass production. Faces, bodies, legs, shoes and hands were manufactured separately and put together. Once the basic parts were joined together, workers took

additional clay to form the details such as shoelaces and armour bindings. Special care was lavished on the heads. Eyebrows, hair and moustaches were neatly formed and attached. No two soldiers look alike. The figures were then fired at 900–1,050 degrees C (1,652–1,922 degrees F. Finally the army was painted with vivid colours based on lacquer. The majority of the soldiers have lost their colouring, but traces of the wonderful painting are still visible.

Above: Terracotta soldier and horse from the Tomb of Qin Shi Huangdi

Left: Terracotta soldiers in rows

Sanchi

WHERE IS IT?
Bhopal district, Madhya Pradesh (India), 9km (5.5 miles) southwest of Vidisha, 70km (43 miles) from Bhopal

WHEN TO VISIT
Best visited October to March

GENERAL INFO
Accessible by road and rail, situated about 1km (0.6 mile) from Sanchi railway station

SANCHI

THE MAURYAN EMPEROR ASHOKA IS CREDITED WITH THE CONSTRUCTION OF 84,000 STUPAS (RELIC MOUNDS) AS PLACES OF VENERATION CONTAINING CORPOREAL RELICS OF THE BUDDHA. ONE WAS ENLARGED SOME CENTURIES LATER TO CREATE THE MAGNIFICENT GREAT STUPA AT SANCHI.

This monument forms part of a complex of Buddhist monasteries, temples and stupas set atop a hill. Ashoka's original stupa was erected in the 3rd century BC; in the 2nd century the Shungas, successors to the Mauryas, encased the stupa with stone slabs and added a railing. Other structures were added to the complex up into the 13th century AD. Thereafter the site was deserted, Buddhism having largely been abandoned in its original homeland.

AN ETERNAL MOUND

In contrast to other early stupas, the stone slabs of Sanchi Great Stupa are undecorated, as is the massive stone railing that surrounds it. The lower part, a cylindrical drum, measures 36m (118ft) in diameter. A double staircase leads up to a balustraded berm used for *pradakshina* (circumambulation), an Indian ritual of veneration. From here rises the hemispherical dome, crowned by a small square railing enclosing the *yashti* (pole) representing the World Axis, surmounted by three *chattras* (umbrellas) symbolizing royalty but also protection and honour for the stupa and its relics.

Four staggered entrances break the circle of the railing at the cardinal points, creating a swastika (an auspicious sign) in plan. At each a magnificent ceremonial *torana* (gateway) was erected at a later date: first the south gateway, the votive gift of the Satavahana king Satakarni (*r*AD11–29), with the north, east and west gateways soon following.

A TREASURY OF BUDDHIST ART

The *toranas* are lavishly decorated with carvings. Each comprises two huge square-section pillars supporting three massive architraves, separated by further pillar segments. The architraves are slightly

Left: General view of the the Great Stupa, at Sanchi

Right: Details of the north gateway: demons assail the Buddha and a *jataka* story set in a forest

curved and terminate at each end in a tightly coiled spiral. Voluptuous female tree-deities, languidly draped around the branches of their trees, support the ends of the lowest architraves, while the pillar capitals are formed of groups of other figures, dwarves on the west gateway, lions on the south and elephants on the east

and north. On the inner face of the pillars are large figures of *dvarapalas* (gate guardians) protecting the entrance. Every other surface on the pillars is divided into panels, the majority illustrating scenes from the Buddha's life and from *jataka* stories (moral tales about the deeds of the Buddha in former incarnations).

SCENES FROM BUDDHA'S LIFE

The panels depict Buddha's departure from his father's kingdom in search of enlightenment and demons futilely tempting the Buddha to abandon his meditations. Others show events after his enlightenment. Also illustrated is the terrible conflict between rival kings to gain control of the Buddha's body after his death at the age of 80. In all these scenes the Buddha is represented by an appropriate symbol: only later did doctrinal changes allow him to be shown in person.

WHERE IS IT?

Near Hospet, Karnataka, southern India

WHEN TO VISIT

Best visited in the winter months, November to February

GENERAL INFO

Accessible by bus from Hospet. Hire a bicycle or moped at the site to tour the extensive ruins

VIJAYANAGARA

BUILT WITHIN AN EXTRAORDINARY LANDSCAPE OF HILLS THAT LOOK LIKE PEBBLES THROWN DOWN BY GIANTS, THE ROYAL CITY OF VIJAYANAGARA (MODERN HAMPI) WAS IN ITS DAY ONE OF THE LARGEST METROPOLISES IN THE WORLD.

Vijayanagara, 'City of Victory', was founded by Hindu princes who threw off Muslim rule around AD1336, carving out an empire that controlled all India south of the Tungabhadra River until its defeat in the disastrous Battle of Talikota in 1565. The sprawling city extends over more than 26sq km (10sq miles), including many of the surrounding modern settlements. Sections of monumental walls survive: traditionally there were seven concentric enclosure walls, the outer ones protecting farmland, while the city lay within the inner four. Canals and aqueducts supplied irrigation water to the fields.

THE ROYAL CENTRE

The walled Royal Centre, home of the royal household, lies on the western side of the city's urban core (the elite residential area), south of the Tungabhadra. At its centre is the Hazara Rama temple, the rulers' personal shrine. A large enclosure to its south was probably used during festivals; it included the Great Platform (the king's viewing platform), carved with scenes from daily royal life.

Just outside the complex are the imposing Elephant Stables. The arched doorways of its 11 alternately domed and vaulted chambers open onto a large *maidan* (parade ground). To its north a building with a raised arcade probably served as a royal stand from which to observe parades.

THE VITTHALA TEMPLE

South of the river a colonnaded street leads up to the magnificent Vitthala (Vishnu) temple, set in a walled precinct entered on three sides through *gopuras* (enormous elaborately carved, tiered gateways). Beautiful decorated pillars support the temple's roof, many carved in the form of rearing animals. The precinct also contains a wonderful temple on wheels: a stone version of the temple cars (chariots) used to carry sacred images in procession.

Left: The many temples at Vijayanagara are exuberantly decorated with relief carvings of gods and animals

Far left: One of the *mandapas* that lie along the Hampi Bazaar, set in the characteristic boulder landscape

THE IMPORTANCE OF RAMA

Reliefs decorating the Hazara Rama temple show elephants, dancing girls and other participants in a procession during the annual Mahanavami festival. Others tell the story of Rama, immortalized in the great Indian epic, the Ramayana. The Vijayanagara region was identified with Kishkindha, the kingdom of the monkeys who aided Rama. Many localities were venerated for their part in Rama's sojourn here.

Right: Stone *ratha* (temple car), at the shrine of Garuda, in the precinct of the Vitthala temple

Below: A general view of the Virapaksha temple

THE SACRED CENTRE

Between the Vitthala temple and the Royal Centre lies the Sacred Centre, dominated by the Virapaksha (Shiva) temple, an ancient shrine still used in worship. The temple compound stands at the head of the Hampi Bazaar, a paved and colonnaded street flanked by stone buildings. Also within the Sacred Centre are smaller shrines and monolithic sculptures, including a magnificent Nandi bull.

AFTERMATH

After the empire fell, Vijayanagara was sacked, a process that lasted more than six months, and thereafter it was largely deserted. Since the 1970s the site has been intensively studied, with some excavation taking place and very detailed recording of the surviving structures.

MOHENJO-DARO

THE VISITOR TO MOHENJO-DARO STEPS BACK MORE THAN 4,000 YEARS TO WALK ALONG BROAD STREETS AND NARROW LANES STILL FLANKED BY BRICK BUILDINGS SEVERAL STOREYS HIGH. WHEN THE HARAPPANS LIVED HERE, THESE WALLS PROBABLY BORE DAZZLING WHITE PLASTER, PERHAPS WITH PAINTED PATTERNS.

Mohenjo-Daro

WHERE IS IT?
Larkana district, Sindh, not far from the Indus River (Pakistan)

WHEN TO VISIT
During the winter months

GENERAL INFO
Probably the largest city of the Indus (Harappan) civilization, which flourished 2600–1800BC. Accessible by air, train and road

Drains capped with stone slabs run along the streets, taking the waste water from every house, most furnished with a tiled bathroom and many with a toilet, a remarkable feature for the time. Fresh water was supplied from wells, to which another course of bricks was added each time the street level was raised: now, after metres of later deposits have been removed, they are left towering above the visitor. Mohenjo-daro is thought originally to have had around 700 wells to supply its inhabitants, perhaps numbering 100,000.

A GREAT CITY

Only the central part of Mohenjo-daro has been excavated: most of its 250ha (618acres) are still buried under metres of silt deposited over the millennia by the annual flooding of the nearby Indus River. On the east side of the excavated area were many industrial premises where shell, stone, metal and clay were worked to make the fine pottery, jewellery and stone and metal tools used by the Harappans. Most buildings in the Lower Town, the eastern of the city's two mounds, are well-appointed houses, each constructed around a courtyard where much of daily life took place. Access via a passage from the street ensured privacy. From the courtyard opened the bathroom and other rooms, some probably for storage. A stairway led to one or several upper storeys and the roof, where people could sleep on hot nights.

Mohenjo-daro was a planned city, constructed around 2600–2500BC on two massive mounds of mud and sand within thick mud-brick revetments, raising the buildings above potential flooding.

THE CITADEL

The western mound (the 'Citadel') held many of the city's public buildings. Foremost among these is the Great Bath, a brick-built rectangular pool, made watertight with bitumen, set in a carefully secluded courtyard with bathrooms opening off it. A well supplied water for the pool, which was emptied through a superbly engineered corbelled drain. This was perhaps the venue for religious ceremonies, probably exclusively attended by priests and the city's elusive rulers. Buildings to its south included a possible state warehouse and a pillared hall where other ceremonies may have been conducted.

A LOST WORLD

Mohenjo-daro was abandoned in the early 2nd millennium BC, a time when other Indus cities also declined. History forgot the Harappans and it was not until the 1920s that investigation of a Buddhist stupa at Mohenjo-daro and excavations in the Punjab at Harappa suddenly revealed the existence of the Indus civilization and its magnificent cities.

Left: The Citadel, looking across to the later stupa

Below: A seal bearing the most common design, a unicorn, and an inscription in undeciphered script

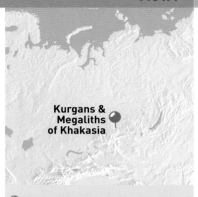

Kurgans & Megaliths of Khakasia

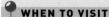

WHERE IS IT?

The Republic of Khakasia is in southern Siberia (Russia); the sites are situated around its capital, Abakan

WHEN TO VISIT

Best from May to September

GENERAL INFO

Excursions to the kurgans with megaliths are being organized by many tour agencies in Abakan; there are collections of decorated megaliths in the museums of Abakan, Minusinsk and in the open-air museum in the village of Poltakov

KURGANS & MEGALITHS OF KHAKASIA

KHAKASIA IS THE RICHEST AREA IN RUSSIA FOR ARCHAEOLOGICAL SITES; THE MOST FAMOUS AND MOST VISIBLE ARE THE STONE STATUES AND THE BIG BURIAL MOUNDS SURROUNDED BY A PERIMETER OF STONE SLABS AND MEGALITHS.

Khakasia is often referred to as an archaeological Mecca. This area, with all kinds of landscapes—from endless steppes to impassable taiga and rocky-mountains—and with its continental climate, has always been attractive to many different tribes and peoples, who left all kinds of archaeological sites here. The most characteristic feature of Khakasian archaeology is the use of stone slabs for the construction of graves and kurgans (burial mounds). Some cultures are distinguished by their love of huge megalithic funerary constructions. In particular, the populous Tagar culture, which inhabited the region in the 7th–2nd centuries BC, occupied all of Khakasia with cemeteries that sometimes contain hundreds of kurgans. The Tagar kurgans consisted of pyramidal constructions made of turf and clay inside a perimeter, built of stone slabs with menhirs (standing stones) at the corners and on the sides. Centuries have passed, and the earthen mounds have eroded, but the stone constructions and the menhirs still remain.

STEPPE IDOLS

A century ago, megalithic statues were still as characteristic a feature of the historical landscape of Khakasia as the kurgans. Now nearly all of them are in museums. These mysterious monuments, dubbed 'steppe idols' by 18th-century travellers and scholars, are usually 2–5m (6.5–16ft) tall, made of sandstone and granite. Carved by the skilful artists of the Okunev culture, they existed in the region during the Early Bronze Age. They usually have a sabre-like shape, with a face in the middle. Realistic human faces are rare, and normally one sees anthropomorphous masks decorated with lines, curves, a third eye, animal horns and ears, and with a complicated headdress. There are often solar symbols, and faces surrounded by solar rays.

EXCAVATION

Between 2004 and 2005, near Salbyk, another royal kurgan was excavated. This kurgan on the natural boundary named Barsuchij Log was also the biggest in its cemetery with a mound 9m (29.5ft) high and 75m (246ft) in diameter. It was robbed in antiquity but the purpose was to study the methods and construction sequence of this complex. This kurgan is 54m (177ft) square, and its stone stelae are up to 3.5m (11.5ft) high beautifully decorated with petroglyphs.

Left: Barsuchy Log Kurgan during excavation

Right: Stelae at Safronov cemetery

DECORATED STELAE

The slabs and megaliths used in the construction of Khakasian kurgans are often decorated with pecked and engraved images. Sometimes the builders re-used statues and stelae taken from sanctuaries or cemeteries of earlier peoples. In other cases the images were made for the burial or the kurgan and often the people of later cultures pecked the depictions on the visible stone surfaces. These open-air galleries occur everywhere in Khakasia, but the most impressive is the Safronov cemetery. Its decorated kurgan slabs are the biggest in Khakasia and indeed Siberia. The cemetery is of the Tagar culture, and the petroglyphs were pecked on its slabs both during the Tagar culture and in later periods. They depict animals, people, birds, concentric circles and various symbols and signs.

GREAT SALBYK

Most of the kurgans of the Tagar culture are a few metres in circumference and the corner stones about 1m (3,28ft) high. As the culture developed, larger kurgans with more and bigger megaliths were built for collective burials and for nobles. The most famous concentration of such kurgans is the Salbyk valley, where among 100 Tagar kurgans there are 15 whose diameter exceeds 50m (164ft). The biggest is the Great Salbyk, excavated in the 1950s. Now one can see only its impressive stone construction, which is a square with sides of 70m (230ft), made of gigantic slabs of Devonian sandstone. At the corners, along the sides and by the entrance, 23 huge vertical stone slabs were set up, which are up to 6m (20ft) high and weigh up to 50 tons. The mound was originally pyramidal in shape, and 25–30m (82–98ft) high. The chamber (5sq m/16sq ft, at a depth of 1.8m/5.9ft) was a complicated construction of logs, birch bark and clay. The vertical stones for the perimeter were brought from far away and it was calculated 100 people working for seven years had constructed the mound, undertaken to bury an elderly chief with his retainers or relatives. The tomb had been ravaged and the only finds were a bronze knife dating to the 5th–4th centuries BC, and a big clay vessel.

TOMSKAYA PISANITSA

A ROCK ON THE RIVER TOM COVERED WITH PETROGLYPHS CARVED 4,000 YEARS AGO IS ONE OF THE MOST INTERESTING ROCK ART SITES OF SIBERIA, ALSO FAMOUS FOR ITS LONG HISTORY OF INVESTIGATION.

Tomskaya Pisanitsa

WHERE IS IT?
In the Kemerovo region of Siberia (Russia), 60km (37 miles) from the city of Kemerovo

WHEN TO VISIT
Any time of the year; closed Mondays and Tuesdays

GENERAL INFO
The rock art site is the centre of a museum reserve with many other archaeological, ethnographical and natural features

Siberia—the vast Asian part of Russia—is incredibly rich in rock art sites, especially in its southwestern part. Hundreds of them, with thousands of figures pecked, engraved or painted on to rock outcrops, are located along almost all the rivers. Russians who came to Siberia in the 16th–17th centuries were impressed with the ancient imagery; they called the decorated rocks Pisanitsas from the Russian word *Pisanyi* which means 'decorated, covered with drawings'. So, in modern language, Tomskaya Pisanitsa means 'Rock art site on the river Tom'.

THE HISTORY

Large carved figures on this scenic rock, facing the river and surrounded by beautiful pine forests, attracted the attention of the first explorers in the 17th century, and an excited description has survived in a chronicle from about 1645. In the early 18th century scholarly investigation of the site began, and since then many famous travellers and scholars, from both Europe and Russia, made frequent visits to the rock on the River Tom and published their descriptions, thoughts and drawings, so the site has the richest historiography and iconography of all Asian rock art sites. From the 1960s to the 1970s the petroglyphs were documented and published, and 20 years ago the site was opened to the public.

THE IMAGERY

The rock surfaces bear about 300 images; the majority of them are gracious figures of running elks, executed with various techniques—pecked, incised or polished—but always in a naturalistic manner with all the important details, such as a typical hook-nosed muzzle, a nicely shaped eye, a dewlap under the head, a hump and long slim criss-crossed legs with cloven hooves; sometimes the heart and aorta are also shown. Some figures are outlines with vertical arched strips on the elks's necks—and nobody knows what they mean. Apart from the elks there are also images of other animals—bears, foxes, does, an owl, a crane, a

heron and a duck; various anthropomorphous figures—fantastic or disguised creatures, a skier, face-masks, phallic dancers, sun-rayed personages; and also boats and numerous symbols and signs. The complicated compositions on the Tom rocks evidently reflect the mythology and beliefs of the tribes inhabiting the area in the Early Bronze Age (late 3rd–early 2nd millennia BC). Similar styles and personages are known in the portable art and on ceramics from dated sites, and also have analogies in the rock art of adjacent areas.

CONTINUING RESEARCH

Despite three centuries of study, discoveries are still being made at Tomskaya Pisanitsa. The making of precise copies with modern methods, such as facsimile imprints, exact tracing onto transparent plastic sheets, photography in oblique light, etc, is producing surprising results. New images between those already known have been revealed, as well as some significant details in the known images. For example, it turned out that some pecked anthropomorphous personages have sunrays around their head; these were engraved with thin lines which had become barely visible with time. Such discoveries are changing our perceptions about the meaning of the petroglyphs, and clarifying their chronological and cultural attribution.

THE MUSEUM

Tomskaya Pisanitsa is located in a picturesque site not far from the city, and has become a favourite place for visitors. Now the whole area is a museum-reserve, also named Tomskaya Pisanitsa, with many interesting features to see, such as a whole replica village of the aboriginal Shor people, a Museum of the Rock Art of Asia, reconstructions of ancient dwellings and burials, a mini-zoo, and many other things.

Above: The rock with petroglyphs above the River Tom is accessible to the public in both summer and winter

Left: The dominant motif of ancient Siberian rock art is the elk—Tomskaya Pisanitsa has about 100 of them

Gyeongju

WHERE IS IT?
Gyeongju, in southeast South Korea

WHEN TO VISIT
Any time of the year. Open:
Heavenly Horse tomb summer
9–6, winter 9–5; Anapji Pond 8–7
(Nov–Feb 8–6); Observatory 9–10

GENERAL INFO
Allow at least one day. The town
centre is easily walkable, with
access to tombs, fortress walls,
ruins and museums within a few
minutes

GYEONGJU

THE GYEONGJU HISTORIC AREA (ALSO SPELLED KYONGJU OR GYONGJU) MAY BE CONSIDERED AN OUTDOOR MUSEUM. DESIGNATED AS WORLD CULTURAL HERITAGE BY UNESCO IN DECEMBER 2000, IT CONTAINS BUDDHIST RELICS, IMPERIAL PALACES AND TOMBS AND GARDENS, PRESERVING THE CULTURE AND HISTORY OF THE OLD CAPITAL OF THE SILLA DYNASTY (AD57–935).

The Daereungwon Tomb Park includes more than 20 large and small tombs of kings and court officials from the Silla period. The dimensions of the tombs vary, with heights ranging from less than 1m (3.28ft) to 23m (75.5ft), most of them with an earthen mound.

Double-shaped tombs were joint burials of a husband and wife. Of these, the Hwangnam Daechong tomb is the biggest. The 59,000 relics excavated reveal the elaborate burial custom. Some of the objects brought to light bear witness to trade with Central Asian countries and the Silk Road.

SPLENDOUR OF THE SILLA

One of the tombs belongs to King Mich'u (r262–284), the 13th king of the Silla Dynasty. The king made Silla a powerful country and defended it from invasions. An ancient legend relating to the tomb tells of soldiers with bamboo leaves in their ears coming out of the king's tomb to defeat his enemies. The tomb is thus called Chukhyonnung or Bamboo Soldier Tomb. The Cheonmachong (Tomb of the Heavenly Horse) is the only one open to public. It received its name from the picture of a flying white horse painted on a saddle flap, which was excavated from the tomb in 1973. The mound is 12.7m (41.6ft) high and 47m (154ft) in diameter. The tomb was built by placing a wooden coffin and a wooden chest for funerary objects on the flat floor and erecting a wooden chamber over them. Boulders were piled on top, and an earthen mound protected the vulnerable structure inside. This tomb is presumed to have been built in AD4–6, and it contained precious gold crowns, gold belts with jade pendants, a leather harness and saddle, pottery and

bronze objects. Some of the artefacts found during the excavation are displayed here, although most are replicas of the original pieces on display at the Gyeongju National Museum.

ICE AND STARS

This ice storage house (Seogbinggo) was built during the Choson period (1392–1910). The Samkukyusa (Legends of the Three Kingdoms) mentions that King Jijeung ordered a storage house for ice to be built in the palace grounds to store ice during the summer months. More than 1,000 stones were used for its construction. Cheomseongdae, the Star Gazing Tower, is known as the oldest observatory in the Far East, built in 634. It has 27 levels of stones in a round shape with four sets of parallel bars to make a square-shaped structure on the top.

WATER AND MOUND

King Munmu (r661–681) built Anapji in 674 as a pleasure garden, with a pond and three islets based on Daoist ideology. He designed it so that it is not possible to view the entire pond at once. In 1975 when the pond was drained for repairs, workers found a wealth of treasures that had been underwater. Theses relics are now in the National Museum.

Left: Artefacts from the Tomb of the Heavenly Horse displayed in the Gyeongju National Museum

Below: Daereungwon Tomb Park, a collection of tombs belonging to kings and court officials from the Silla period

ANURADHAPURA

A JEWEL OF A CITY, SET AMONG GARDENS AND LAKES,
ANURADHAPURA WAS THE FOREMOST SETTLEMENT OF SRI
LANKA FROM THE TIME OF ITS LEGENDARY FOUNDATION BY
PRINCE VIJAYA, WHO TRADITIONALLY INVADED FROM WESTERN
INDIA IN THE 6TH CENTURY BC, UNTIL AD1017 WHEN IT WAS
REPLACED AS CAPITAL BY POLONNARUWA.

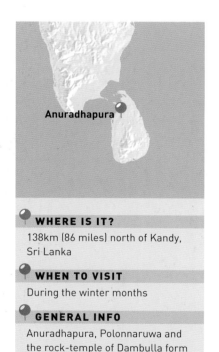

Anuradhapura

WHERE IS IT?

138km (86 miles) north of Kandy,
Sri Lanka

WHEN TO VISIT

During the winter months

GENERAL INFO

Anuradhapura, Polonnaruwa and
the rock-temple of Dambulla form
the renowned Cultural Triangle,
which also contains the rock
fortress of Sigiriya

By the 3rd century BC Anuradhapura was a thriving
city. Mahinda, son of the Indian emperor Ashoka, came
here on a successful mission to convert the inhabitants
to Buddhism. His sister followed, bringing a slip of
the Bodhi tree under which the Buddha had gained
enlightenment. This grew into a tree that is reputedly
still living.

BUDDHIST ESTATES

Sri Lanka's king, Devanampiyatissa, gifted substantial
areas of the city and its environs to the Buddhist
community for monasteries and stupas. The first
shrine, Thuparama, was built to house Ashoka's
generous gift of the Buddha's collarbone and begging
bowl. Pillars originally supported a wooden roof over
the stupa, which, unlike Indian examples, has a conical
spire. Thuparama formed part of the first monastic
complex, the Mahavihara, situated in what had been
Devanampiyatissa's pleasure garden. The king also
created the Mahapali, a wooden alms hall where food
was provided daily for the monks; its only surviving
traces are the stumps of stone columns from its
ground floor pillared hall.

**Right: The magnificent elephant wall built in the 8th century
AD around the Ruvanvel Dagoba**

GUARDSTONES

Guardstones with fine relief carvings of supernatural beings, particularly Nagas (snake deities), flanked the entrance to buildings as protective doorkeepers. Other carved slabs, known as moonstones, were laid at the threshold; these bear a semicircle of auspicious symbols, comprising a goose, and a lion, a horse, a bull and an elephant, respectively representing the zenith and the four cardinal directions.

Dutthagamini, who won control of the island from Tamil invaders in the 1st century BC, was also a notable patron of Buddhism: He founded the Ruvanveli Dagoba (Great Stupa) and built a nine-storey wooden palace, the Lohapasada, richly decorated with carvings, for the Buddhist monks. Later kings endowed other shrines and monasteries.

WATER, WATER EVERYWHERE

Anuradhapura lies within the Dry Zone, the area of Sri Lanka in which irrigation is essential for agriculture, promoting the early development of sophisticated hydraulic engineering. By the 4th century BC, the people of the city were constructing large tanks (reservoirs) and canals and by the 3rd had developed a discharge system employing a valve-pit sluice. Three large tanks were created to the west of the city, and an enormous reservoir to the southeast, while smaller pleasure lakes and pools were built within the city itself. That within the Isurumaniya monastery had decorative carvings on its surrounding rocks, including elephants, which seem to be playing in the water.

LOST CITY

After its abandonment, Anuradhapura was swallowed up by jungle. From the 19th century AD, however, its Buddhist shrines were again brought into use for worship and the vegetation began to be cleared. The first of many excavations began in 1890, uncovering the city's Buddhist past. In recent years investigations have revealed pre-urban settlements and traces of the city's domestic architecture.

Left: Flanking guardstones and a moonstone protect the entrance to this building at Anuradhapura

Below: The Kuttampokuna, one of a pair of twin bathing pools within the Abhayagiri monastery

Above: A guardstone depicting a Naga bearing a flowering branch and a vase of flowers, symbols of prosperity

Right: Standing Buddha and worshipper at Anuradhapura

BOĞHAZKÖY

THE HITTITE EMPIRE, KNOWN AS THE 'LAND OF A THOUSAND GODS', WAS ONE OF THE MAJOR POWERS IN THE ANCIENT NEAR EAST. THE REMAINS OF ITS CAPITAL, HATTUŞAŞ, CONTINUE TO INSPIRE AWE, AND GIVE THE VISITOR AN APPRECIATION OF THE MEASURES TAKEN BY THE HITTITES TO SAFEGUARD THEIR CAPITAL FROM ATTACK.

WHERE IS IT?
Close to the village of Boğazkale (formerly known as Boğhazköy) in central Turkey, approximately 200km (124 miles) east of Ankara

GENERAL INFO
If you do not have your own transport, there are hourly buses from Ankara to Sungurlu; from there is it possible to catch a shared taxi or minibus for the one-hour drive to the site. A joint ticket for admission to Hattuşaş and Yazılıkaya (a Hittite cult site with famous relief carvings) is available

The site has a strategic position at the head of a wide, fertile valley, and its occupation began from about 2500BC, when it was a merchant colony. However,

Hattuşaş gained prominence from the 17th century BC onwards, when it was adopted as capital of the newly-founded Hittite dynasty. The city was at its height from about 1400 to 1200BC, when the Hittite empire fell, although the citadel survived and was re-occupied. The main places of interest on this immense site are the Büyük Mabet (Great Temple), close to the entrance to the site, three city gates in the southern part of the site and the Büyük Kale (Great Fortress).

THE CITY GATES
To appreciate the scale of the site, it is worth following the path inside the restored city walls to see the three gates to Hattuşaş situated at the south of the site—the Aslanıkapı (the Lion Gate), the Yerkapı (the Earth Gate, popularly known as the Sphinx Gate) and the Kralkapı (the King's Gate, which actually shows the weather god Teshuba). The sculptures on the Aslanıkapı and Kralkapı are copies of the originals, which are now in Ankara, but give a good idea of the original appearance. The sphinxes from the inner part of the Yerkapı are also in museums, but traces of one of the original sphinxes on the outside of the gate remain.

THE GREAT FORTRESS
The Büyük Kale (Great Fortress) was the fortified palace of the Hittite rulers and enjoyed an extremely strategic position, easily defensible from all sides.

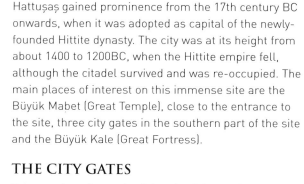

The fortress consisted of three courtyards situated at different levels, the uppermost being the palace itself.

HITTITE GODS AND GODDESSES

The best-preserved surviving Hittite temple is the Büyük Mabet (Great Temple) at Hattuşaş, even though only the foundations survive. It is dedicated to the two most important Hittite deities, the weather god Teshuba and the sun goddess Hebut. Other deities frequently depicted in Hittite art are the sun god Kusuh and Sharruma, the son of Hebut. Almost a thousand other deities were part of the Hittite pantheon, many of which were incorporated from other societies conquered by the Hittites.

Above: The Aslanıkapı (the Lion Gate), one of the three gates to the city

Left: The Büyük Mabet (Great Temple)

THE HITTITE ARCHIVES

Arguably the most important finds from Hattuşaş are the group of some 3,000 clay tablets inscribed with the cuneiform script, found close to one of the entrances to the Great Fortress. These tablets have provided invaluable historical information on Hittite society and politics. Probably the most significant is a peace treaty signed in about 1270BC by the Hittite king Hattusilis III and the Egyptian pharaoh Ramesses II.

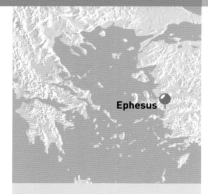

Ephesus

EPHESUS

ONE OF THE LEADING CLASSICAL CITIES OF ASIA MINOR FAMOUS FOR ITS TEMPLE OF ARTEMISIS, WHICH IS NOW SEVERAL MILES INLAND DUE TO THE SILTING UP OF ITS HARBOUR. THE THREE MAIN AREAS ARE THE CITY, THE SANCTUARY OF ARTEMIS AND THE CHURCH OF ST. JOHN AT AYASOLUK.

WHERE IS IT?
Inland from the modern harbour of Kusadasi and near the modern town of Selçuk in Turkey. The archaeological museum is located in Selçuk

GENERAL INFO
Open all year but there are restricted opening times to main archaeological site and museum. For further information www. kultur.gov.tr

The Artemision, or Temple of Artemis, was one of the Seven Wonders of the ancient world, with the earliest temple probably constructed in the sixth century BC. The length of the building was around 115m (377ft), the central building surrounded by some 127 columns in multiple layers. This temple was destroyed by fire in 356BC, which coincided with the birth of Alexander the Great. Work on the replacement started after Alexander's visit to the city in 334.

THE THEATRE

The theatre cut into the side of the hillside continues to dominate the ancient city. It was probably constructed in the Hellenistic period and adapted during the reigns of the Roman emperors Claudius (AD41–54) and Trajan (AD98–117). Some 24,000 people could probably have been seated in the auditorium, which is over 145m (476ft) wide. The theatre was the setting for the great riot prompted by the preaching of the apostle Paul and described in the Acts of the Apostles. A major road ran westwards from the theatre towards the harbour. The harbour gymnasium and bathing complex lay to one side of the road.

Left: The main city of Ephesus

Right: Column drum depicting a female figure standing between a winged youth, probably Thanatos (Death), and Hermes, from the later Temple of Artemis

Next spread: An inscription covers a pillar near the Library of Celsus

TEMPLE OF ARTEMIS
The temple was excavated by the British archaeologist David Hogarth (1862–1927) in 1904–05. Architectural fragments from the temple can be seen in the British Museum. Other finds from the Austrian excavations can be found in Vienna.

THE LIBRARY OF CELSUS

A monumental building lay at the foot of the road leading to the upper agora. This dual-purpose structure served as a tomb for Gaius Julius Celsus Polemaeanus and as a library. It was constructed by Celsus' son and heir, Gaius Julius Aquila, in AD110. Details of the benefaction were recorded in an inscription displayed on the building. The library was housed on three levels.

THE UPPER AGORA

This public area contained some of the administrative buildings for the city; the *bouleuterion* was the meeting place for the city's council (or *boule*) and could seat some 1,400 individuals in its semicircular structure.

THE CHURCH OF ST. JOHN

A second-century Christian work, The Acts of John, linked Ephesus to the apostle John, Jesus' 'beloved disciple'. By the fourth century AD a church had been erected on the site of his supposed burial on the hill of Ayasoluk to the north of the main city. This was replaced by the Byzantine emperor Justinian I (527–565) in the sixth century by a grand basilica; his other projects included Ayia Sophia in Istanbul and also the basilica at Ravenna, Italy.

Above: St. John's Christian basilica, Ayasoluk

Left: Roman theatre at Ephesus

Far left: The Library of Celsus

PERGAMOM

THE HELLENISTIC ROYAL CAPITAL OF THE ATTALID DYNASTY WAS INTENDED TO EVOKE THE GLORIES OF FIFTH-CENTURY BC ATHENS. AFTER THE DEATH OF ALEXANDER THE GREAT, HIS EMPIRE WAS DIVIDED INTO SMALLER KINGDOMS; THE ATTALID DYNASTY EMERGED IN NORTHWESTERN TURKEY WITH THEIR CAPITAL AT PERGAMOM.

WHERE IS IT?
In western Turkey, near the modern town of Bergama

GENERAL INFO
Open all year. The main acropolis is very steep

The Attalids used Periclean Athens as their model to create a stunning city on the side of the mountain. At the top of the city were the royal palaces. Many of the monuments celebrated the defeat of the Gauls in central Anatolia (Galatia), and developed the theme of civilization defeating the barbarians. The main kings associated with the development were Eumenes II (197–159BC) and Attalos II (159–138BC). Pergamom was bequeathed to Rome on the death of Attalos III in 133BC.

THE SANCTUARY OF ATHENA

One of the focal points for the city was the Temple of Athena that stood on the edge of the hill overlooking the theatre. Pergamom, like Athens, had Athena as its patron deity. It stood in a large courtyard flanked by colonnades on which the trophies of war were carved. In the open space there appears to have been a series of monuments celebrating the victory over the Gauls. A Roman copy of one of the statues, *The Dying Gaul*, can be seen in Rome.

The famous Pergamene library was adjacent to the sanctuary of Athena. This probably contained several hundred thousand works. Inside the library was found a large marble copy of the Athena Parthenos from Athens.

THE ALTAR OF ZEUS

At the southern end of the acropolis was a massive stepped altar facing the steep edge. It was surrounded by a continuous frieze that runs round the outside. The altar was approached from the east, and as you

Left: Pergamom ruins

processed to the front, you would be able to view the battle between the Olympian gods and the giants (an allusion to the defeat of the Gauls). At the heart of the altar, at the top of the steps and within a colonnade, was a further frieze showing the foundation myth of the city.

THE THEATRE

The theatre was located on a steeply sloping site and helps to direct the eye to the different buildings on the acropolis. It probably could have seated some 10,000 people in 80 rows. At one end of the north to south terrace was a small temple of Dionysos standing on a high podium.

THE SANCTUARY OF ASKLEPIOS

The sanctuary of the healing god Asklepios was sited in the lower city. This was a rival to the sanctuary at Epidauros in Greece. Excavations have revealed remains of a circular structure in the southeast corner of the sanctuary where those who were ill could be placed for treatment. In the eastern range of buildings was the temple constructed by the Roman benefactor L. Cuspius Pactumeius Rufinus in the middle of the second century BC. It was designed as a small-scale replica of the Pantheon in Rome.

Right: Hellenistic theatre

RELIEFS

Excavated by the German Carl Humann in the 1870s, the stone reliefs from the Altar of Zeus (see left) are now displayed in the Pergamom Museum in Berlin.

TROY (HISARLIK)

THE CITY OF TROY, IMMORTALIZED BY HOMER IN THE ILIAD, HAS BEEN THE INSPIRATION FOR MANY OTHER WRITERS AND ARTISTS THROUGHOUT TIME. ALTHOUGH THE LOCATION HAS BEEN DISPUTED, HISARLIK IS USUALLY IDENTIFIED AS HOMER'S TROY.

Troy (Hisarlik)

WHERE IS IT?

Commanding the Dardanelles, adjacent to the Gallipoli beaches (Turkey). There is regular minibus access to the site from the town of Çanakkale, which is 32km (20 miles) to the northeast

GENERAL INFO

The site is open all year. Although there is a small visitor centre, there is no museum at the site. Many of the finds from Troy are exhibited in Berlin, and the well-known collection of jewellery, modelled by Sophia Schliemann for a famous photograph and known as the Treasure of Priam, is in Moscow

The first excavations at Hisarlik were undertaken by Heinrich Schliemann between 1871 and 1873, one of the first deliberate excavations of an archaeological site. All visible traces of the Troy known from legend had disappeared, seemingly lost forever, until Schliemann gained permission to excavate the mound of Hisarlik in the late 19th century. Twentieth-century excavations by Manfred Korfmann have proved that the city of Troy was much larger than the mound itself.

TROY THROUGH THE AGES

Troy was continuously occupied for approximately 4,500 years, from about 3000BC onwards. The settlement that Schliemann believed to be Homer's Troy dates to *c*2500–2300BC, and was destroyed by a catastrophic fire. A city dating to the late 13th/early 12th century—the time of the Trojan War—also suffered a disastrous fire, although it is uncertain whether it was a consequence of the sack of Troy as related in literature. The Trojan legend attracted visitors in the Hellenistic and Roman periods, just as it does today, and much of the best-preserved visible architecture on the site dates from this era. The Temple of Athena was rebuilt in honour of Alexander the Great after his life was taken by Lysimachus, one of Alexander's generals. Alexander was closely associated with the old Temple of Athena; before his war against the Persian Empire, Alexander had made an offering of his own armour at the temple. The temple was rebuilt again by the Roman

emperor Augustus, in honour of a promise made by his great uncle, Julius Caesar.

THE SITE OF TROY TODAY

As a result of the long occupation of the mound of Hisarlik, and Schliemann's excavation, it can be difficult to gain a coherent impression of the site. Korfmann's team has done much to clarify the interpretation of the various levels of Troy. Perhaps the most spectacular remains are the walls, which date to around 1300BC.

THE TROJAN WAR

The legend of the Trojan War is based on an amalgamation of several ancient sources, most famously the *Iliad* by Homer, but also including works that are substantially lost, such as the *Ilioupersis*, which is an account of the sack of Troy. Although various aspects of the *Iliad* are anachronistic, Homer's

epic poem preserves some elements that have a factual basis, inevitably amended and elaborated through time. The catalyst for the war was the elopement of Paris, prince of Troy, and Helen, wife of Menelaus, king of Sparta. Menelaus and his brother Agamemnon, ruler of Mycenae, mustered a fleet and set sail for Troy. The Greeks besieged Troy for nine years and were involved in heroic struggles with the Trojans. The end of the siege came suddenly when the Greek forces led by wily Odysseus hid inside the Trojan Horse that the Trojans brought into the city. Caught unawares, Priam, king of Troy, was killed and his city laid to waste.

Left: Sanctuary from the Hellenistic period in front of the imposing city walls

Below: The Roman Odeion, where musical and dramatic performances took place

AUSTRALASIA

Left: Petroglyph of tuna fish, Abu Tongariki,
Easter Island

Kakadu

WHERE IS IT?
About 120km (75 miles) east of Darwin, Northern Territory, Australia

WHEN TO VISIT
Wet season flooding (November to April) can restrict access. Guided activities mostly operate during the dry season

GENERAL INFO
Two rock art complexes are open to the public: Nourlangie and Nanguluwurr, and Ubirr

KAKADU NATIONAL PARK

THE SPECTACULAR SANDSTONE CLIFFS OF KAKADU CONTAIN ONE OF THE LARGEST CONCENTRATIONS OF ROCK ART IN THE WORLD. THE PAINTINGS ARE IN A VARIETY OF STYLES AND DOCUMENT ABORIGINAL LIFE IN THE AREA FROM ABOUT 20,000 YEARS AGO TO THE PRESENT DAY.

Kakadu covers nearly 20,000sq km (7,720sq miles) of wetlands, rocky hills or 'stone country', and the sandstone cliffs and gorges of the Arnhem Land escarpment. The rich natural resources of the area have sustained Aboriginal people for thousands of years and some of the earliest evidence of occupation in Australia, dating back perhaps 60,000 years, has been discovered in Nauwalabila and Malakunanja II rock shelters.

KAKADU ROCK ART

The area is best known for its rock art. About 5,000 sites have been documented, but there are believed to be thousands more. The tradition of rock painting in the Kakadu area goes back at least 20,000 years and finds of ochre in the earliest levels of sites suggest even older paintings that have not survived.

Dating rock art can be very difficult. In sites with more than one style these can be given relative ages by studying the order of different layers of painting. There are at least 11 different styles of art in Kakadu sites. The subject matter of paintings can also give clues to dating. For example, extinct animals, such as the thylacine, or Tasmanian tiger, and the Tasmanian devil are portrayed in the older art.

ROCK ART SUBJECT MATTER

The long time span of occupation at Kakadu means that the environment has undergone significant changes. These changes affected the prehistoric way of life and are reflected in the rock art. During the last Ice Age, before about 8,000 years ago, the climate was much drier and sea levels were lower. Art of this period has many naturalistic depictions of land animals and dynamic portrayals of human figures. Rising sea levels at the end of the last Ice Age had significant effects on the environment, with the development of estuarine conditions as far inland as the Arnhem Land escarpment.

Portrayals of land animals became much less common and were replaced by fish and saltwater crocodiles. The colourful X-ray style is the most prominent during this period. These paintings show internal organs and bones of the subject within an outline silhouette. Many paintings from the estuarine period portray ancestral creation figures, which are significant in the mythology of Aboriginal groups in the area today. About 1,500 years ago, estuarine conditions were replaced by freshwater wetlands. The rich resources of the wetlands supported a large Aboriginal population. This change is reflected in the art by depictions of goose hunting and wetland species such as long-necked turtles and waterlilies. The X-ray style continues in a more decorative style, with the outline divided into decorative zones rather than a representation of internal structures.

Above: X-ray style kangaroo painted over a red human figure

Left: People with mythic beings painted by Najombolmi in 1964

WHERE IS IT?

Western New South Wales, Australia; about 110km (68 miles) northeast of Mildura

WHEN TO VISIT

January and February can be extremely hot. Roads may be closed after rain

GENERAL INFO

A visitor's centre provides information about the natural and cultural heritage of the park and self-guided walks and drives. Guided activities are mostly during school holiday periods

Below: The dry bed of Lake Mungo

LAKE MUNGO

LAKE MUNGO, IN FAR WESTERN NEW SOUTH WALES, IS PART OF THE DRIED-UP WILLANDRA LAKES SYSTEM. THE ARCHAEOLOGICAL SITES REVEALED BY EROSION OF CLAY AND SAND DUNES AROUND THE FORMER LAKES PROVIDE A DETAILED RECORD OF HUMAN ADAPTATION TO CHANGING CLIMATES OVER 50,000 YEARS.

The massive crescent-shaped dune, or lunette, on the eastern shore of Lake Mungo is known as 'the Walls of China'. It is thought to have been named by Chinese labourers working in the pastoral industry in the 1860s. The dune sediments are constantly being eroded by wind, bringing to light new archaeological sites. Study of the different layers of sediment in the dunes has allowed a remarkably detailed reconstruction of the climatic history of the area. The archaeological sites provide a fascinating picture of how Aboriginal people adapted to the changes in climate.

SIGNS OF HUMAN SETTLEMENT

Fifty thousand years ago the Willandra Lakes were filled by water from the Lachlan River. As the climate began to dry out, from about 40,000 years ago, the human inhabitants of the region had to adapt their way of life to increasing drought conditions. By 20,000 years ago the lake system was completely dry.

Hearths and earth ovens, middens, scatters of stone artefacts and stone quarries around the lakes provide a vivid picture of life when they were full. People hunted a range of large and small animals, collected frogs, freshwater mussels and crayfish, and fished

for Murray cod and golden perch. Stone from local quarries was used to make tools for chopping, cutting and scraping. Archaeologists have mostly focused on the more ancient sites, but many more recent sites exist scattered across the dunes and the ancient dry lake bed.

HUMAN REMAINS

The most remarkable finds at Lake Mungo are the human remains. Burnt bones found eroding from the lunette in 1968 proved to be those of a young woman who had been cremated on the shores of the lake. Her bones were then gathered and smashed, and finally interred in a small pit. In 1974, a second burial was found. An adult male had been laid in a shallow grave and covered with red ochre. The original radiocarbon dates suggested that the cremation occurred about 25,000 years ago and the burial about 30,000 years ago. In 1999, researchers using new dating methods controversially suggested Mungo Man could be more than 60,000 years old. However, more detailed re-examination of the finds now suggests an age of about 40,000 years for both burials, and dates the earliest human presence in the area, shown by stone tools, at about 50,000 years ago.

ANCIENT PEOPLES OF AUSTRALIA

The first discoveries at Lake Mungo came at a time when archaeologists had only recently demonstrated Ice Age occupation of Australia. They provided an unusual insight into the beliefs of ancient people and therefore have an important place in the history of Australian archaeology. Human remains, the bones of extinct animals and camp sites continue to be discovered and contribute to the remarkably detailed picture of Aboriginal adaptation to changing environments over the last 50,000 years.

Above: Wind-eroded dunes on the 'Walls of China '

 FOOTPRINTS

In 2003, the discovery of over 400 fossilized human footprints added yet another dimension to the archaeological record of the area. A group of men, women and children had walked over the wet mud of a clay pan about 20,000 years ago.

Nan Madol

WHERE IS IT?

Temwen Island, Pohnpei,
Federated States of Micronesia

GENERAL INFO

The ruins can be reached by road
or by boat and tours are available.
For further information see
www.pohnpeiheaven.com/
nanmadol.htm

**Right: Aerial view showing canals
and islets**

**Below: Wall of the Nandauwas tomb
complex**

NAN MADOL

NAN MADOL, ON POHNPEI IN THE CAROLINE ISLANDS, IS PERHAPS THE
MOST SPECTACULAR SITE IN OCEANIA. THE VAST COMPLEX OF ARTIFICIAL
ISLETS WITH CANALS BETWEEN THEM IS SOMETIMES CALLED THE 'VENICE OF
THE PACIFIC'.

Nan Madol comprises an impressive series of ruined
stone structures, including house foundations,
tunnels and underground vaults, built on about 90
artificial islets. The rectangular islets are constructed
of massive columnar basalt stones with coral and
rubble fill on tidal flats and connected by a network of
canals. The whole site covers about 81ha (200 acres) of
sheltered reef and is protected from the sea by massive
sea walls.

THE EARLY DAYS

The first map of Nan Madol was produced in
1910. Since then, archaeologists have mapped the
archaeological remains of more than 20 islets.
Excavations have chronicled the development of Nan
Madol, and established a chronological framework that
can be related to Pohnpei oral history. The site seems
to have been first occupied about 2,000 years ago,
perhaps by Lapita colonists. The main construction
phase, when the artificial islets with their monumental
architecture were built, seems to span several hundred
years. Despite this long period of development, there
appears to have been central planning of the formal
layout. There are two distinct areas: a religious and
ceremonial centre in the northern sector, with an
administrative headquarters to the south.

SAUDELEUR DYNASTY

Nan Madol served as the ceremonial and
administrative centre for the Saudeleur dynasty, which
united the people of Pohnpei under a centralized
monarchy for about 400 years. The artificial islets
provided both residential and tomb complexes for
the ruling elite. The origins of the Saudeleurs are
not known for certain. Pohnpei oral traditions tell us
that they originated with two brothers who arrived on
Pohnpei about AD1200. Centralized Saudeleur rule
seems to have collapsed about AD1600, to be replaced
by regional chiefdoms. By the time Europeans visited
Pohnpei in the 19th century the vast Nan Madol site
had been abandoned. The massive tomb complex of
Nandauwas dominates the site. Its outer walls, made
of enormous basalt slabs with coral rubble infill, rise
more than 7m (23ft) above the level of the canal and
enclose a huge courtyard and burial vaults.

EASTER ISLAND

THE WHOLE OF THIS ISLAND, THE MOST REMOTE
PERMANENTLY INHABITED PLACE IN THE WORLD, IS AN
ARCHAEOLOGICAL SITE AND A SOURCE OF CONSTANT MYSTERY
AND WONDER.

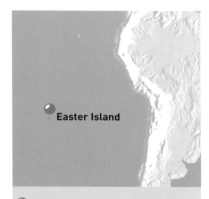

Easter Island

WHERE IS IT?
In the middle of the South Pacific,
to the west of Chile (to which it
belongs)

GENERAL INFO
One can visit from a cruise-ship, or
by flying (a five-hour journey) from
either Santiago de Chile or from
Tahiti, all year round

**Right: The statues on the outer slope
of Rano Raraku are buried up to the
neck in sediment**

Easter Island received its name from the Dutch
commander Jacob Roggeveen, who encountered the
island on Easter Sunday, 5 April 1722. It is now often
called Rapa Nui (big Rapa), because 19th-century
Tahitian sailors thought it looked like a large version
of the island of Rapa. It was first colonized by people
from East Polynesia (probably Mangareva) in the early
centuries AD. They proceeded to produce the most
amazing Stone-Age culture the world has ever known,
with hundreds of massive platforms, up to 1,000
huge statues, a wealth of rock art and its own writing
system.

HUGE STATUES

The platforms (*ahu*) are mostly located around the
coast of this small triangular volcanic island (about
171sq km/66sq miles). They comprise a core of rubble
held in place by a facing of slabs, some of them very
finely cut. The statues (*moai*) were almost all carved
from the soft volcanic tuff at the quarry of Rano
Raraku. Those erected on platforms varied from
2m (6.5ft) to 10m (33ft) in height, and weighed up to
82 tons. They are all variations on a theme: a human
figure with a prominent angular nose and chin, and
often elongated perforated ears containing disks. The
bodies, which end at the abdomen, have arms held
tightly to the sides, and hands held in front, with long
fingertips meeting a stylized loincloth. They represent
ancestor figures.

Previous spread: The recently restored platform of Tongariki with its 15 *moai* of varying sizes

Below: Some of the many birdman petroglyphs at Orongo; on the corner of the rock can be seen the carved face of Makemake, the creator god

ROCK ART

Easter Island also has the richest rock art in the Pacific, with beautiful paintings in caves and drystone houses, and hundreds of fine petroglyphs in caves and the open air. The finest collection of images is found at Orongo, the ceremonial village built on a clifftop between the ocean and the huge crater of Rano Kau. Here the dominant motif is the 'birdman', a half-human frigate bird in a crouching position, often holding an egg.

WRITING SYSTEM

The 'rongorongo' writing system survives only on 25 wooden tablets scattered around the world's museums. Debate still rages as to whether the islanders developed it themselves, or whether it was inspired by their encounter with European writing in the 18th century.

END OF AN ERA

Over centuries, the islanders totally modified their environment, most significantly by cutting down all of its once-dense forest cover. Their earlier way of life eventually collapsed, statues ceased to be carved, and 1,000 years of peaceful co-existence were shattered. Conflict led to the toppling of all the statues, and a new social system arose whereby an annual leader or 'birdman' was chosen by competition.

Right: The fine *moai* on the restored Ahu Nau Nau at Anakena, some of them with red topknots

THE AUTOMOBILE ASSOCIATION WOULD LIKE TO THANK THE FOLLOWING PHOTOGRAPHERS, COMPANIES AND PICTURE LIBRARIES FOR THEIR ASSISTANCE IN THE PREPARATION OF THIS BOOK.

Abbreviations for the picture credits are as follows – (t) top; (b) bottom; (c) centre; (l) left; (r) right; (AA) AA World Travel Library.

1 Paul Bahn; **2** AA/R Strange; **6-7** Photolibrary Group; **8** Kenneth Garrett/National Geographic/Getty Images; **9** Photolibrary Group; **12** © The Gallery Collection/Corbis; **13** Will & Deni McIntyre/Stone/Getty Images; **14** Enrique Lopez; **16/17** Paul Bahn; **17b** AA/P Bennett; **18/19** Yves Marcoux/First Light/Getty Images; **19t** Danita Delimont/Ancient Art & Architecture Collection; 20-26b Photolibrary Group; **26/27** Kenneth Garrett/National Geographic/Getty Images; **28** AA/R Strange; **29** Damian Davies/Photographer's Choice/Getty Images; **30/31** © Danny Lehman/Corbis; **31** Olmec/The Bridgeman Art Library/Getty Images; **32/33, 33** Photolibrary Group; **34** Louis Grandadam/Stone/Getty Images; **35** © Atlantide Phototravel/Corbis; **36/37** R H Productions/Robert Harding World Imagery/Getty Images; **38/39** Photolibrary Group; **40/41** © Pablo Corral Vega/Corbis; **41** Photolibrary Group; **42/43** © Pablo Corral Vega/Corbis; **44/45** AA/G Marks; **46-47** Photolibrary Group; **48** © Charles & Josette Lenars/Corbis; **49** © Yann Arthus-Bertrand/Corbis; **50** Grotte de Pech Merle, Lot, France/Index/The Bridgeman Art Library; **52-53** Photolibrary Group; **54/55** © P Cabrol/Centre de Préhistoire du Pech-Merle; **55** Grotte de Pech Merle, Lot, France/Index/The Bridgeman Art Library; **56-59** Photolibrary Group; **60** AA/A Mockford & N Bonetti; **61** AA/R Surnam; **62/63** AA/A Mockford & N Bonetti; **64** AA/P Wilson; **65** AA/R Surnam; **66/67** AA/T Harris; **67, 68/69** Photolibrary Group; **69** C M Dixon/The Ancient Art & Architecture Collection; **70** Photolibrary Group; **71** The Bridgeman Art Library/Getty Images; **72, 74/75** Photolibrary Group; **73** National Archaeological Museum, Athens, Greece, Giraudon/The Bridgeman Art Library; **75** AA/R Surnam; **76/77, 78** Photolibrary Group; **79** AA/M Short; **80/81** Photolibrary Group; **81** Paul Bahn; **83-84** Photolibrary Group; **85** The Bridgeman Art Library/Getty Images; 86/87 Photolibrary Group; 88-89 AA/N Setchfield; 90 AA/C Sawyer; **91** Photolibrary Group; **92/93, 93** AA/M Jourdan; **94-95, 96/97** Photolibrary Group; **98** © Pixonnet.com/Alamy; **99-101** Photolibrary Group; **102/103** AA/G Matthews; **104/105** AA; 105 AA/R Coulam; **106** AA/E Ellington; **107** AA/S Whitehorn; **109, 110/11** Photolibrary Group; **112** ©NTPL/Joe Cornish; **113** Photolibrary Group; **114/115** AA/I Burgum; **115** AA/M Kipling; **116-119** Photolibrary Group; **120-121** AA/R Strange; **122** Kenneth Garrett/National Geographic/Getty Images; **123** AA/R Strange; **125-126** Photolibrary Group; **127** AA/R Strange; **128/129, 130/131** AA/C Sawyer; **132** Kenneth Garrett/National Geographic/Getty Images; **133** The Bridgeman Art Library/Getty Images; **134** Photolibrary Group; **135** AA/R Strange; **136-139** Photolibrary Group; **139**(inset) Alistair Duncan/Dorling Kindersley/Getty Images; **140/141, 141-145** Photolibrary Group; **146/147** © Nathan Benn/Corbis; **147-171, 172/173** Photolibrary Group; **173** A Beaumont/Ancient Art & Architecture Collection; **174/175, 176/177, 177** Photolibrary Group; **178** Martin Gray/National Geographic/Getty Images; **179** Andrew McConnell/Robert Harding World Imagery/Getty Images; **180/181** Martin Gray/National Geographic/Getty Images; **182/183** Photolibrary Group; **183** M Jelliffe/Ancient Art & Architecture Collection; **184/185, 186/187** Photolibrary Group; **187** © Heini Schneebeli/ The Bridgeman Art Library; **188-191, 192/193** Photolibrary Group; **194-195** Paul Bahn; **196/197, 198** Photolibrary Group; **199** OTHK/Asia Images/Getty Images; **200/201, 201** Photolibrary Group; **202** AA/I Morejohn; **203** AA/A Mockford & N Bonetti; **204-206** AA/B Madison; **207** J Stevens/Ancient Art & Architecture Collection; **208-213, 214/215** Photolibrary Group; **215** The Bridgeman Art Library/Getty Images; **216-218** Elena Miklashevich; **219** Aleksey Kochanovich; **220-230** Photolibrary Group; **231** British Museum, London/The Bridgeman Art Library; **232/233** AA/J F Pin; **234-237** Photolibrary Group; **238/239** © Dennis Cox/Alamy; **239** © Peter Horree/Alamy; **240-243** Photolibrary Group; **244/245** Laura Basell; **245** Danita Delimont/Ancient Art & Architecture Collection; **246** Photolibrary Group; **247** © Jim Sugar/Corbis; **248/249, 250/251** Photolibrary Group; **252** Paul Bahn; **253** Photolibrary Group

Every effort has been made to trace the copyright holders, and we apologise in advance for any accidental errors. We would be happy to apply the corrections in the following edition of this publication.